Purpose

in the

Pain

Tim Wiseman

Purpose in the Pain

"Books for the Journey"
StoneGate Publishing Co., Inc.
Longview 2011

Dedication

"I want to dedicate this book to my Heavenly Father. Without You, I could do nothing.

"I also want to extend my gratitude to Misty, my wife and my best friend. This book could not have been written without your patience, encouragement and support.

"And to the greatest gift God has ever given me, my children: Silas, Malachi and Emma. I love you very much and thanks for letting me be your dad…Ha!

"To my parents who raised me in a Godly home and set the best example before me.

"To my pastor, Marty Strait, thank you for digging deep in the Word of God to teach me truth and for your spiritual covering.

"To my publishers, Bill and Vivian Marie Keith, thank you for believing in me as a writer. Your kind words have been a strong motivation."

Contents

Purpose in the Pain
by Tim Wiseman

Verse 1:

Nothing is out of your reach,
No one can run from your hand;

Your love cannot be escaped,
In Your grace we all stand;

You have a plan for us,
You are our destiny;

You are our God,
You reign in Sovereignty

Chorus:

So no matter what I face,
Or how hard life becomes;

My trust is in You,
Where you brought me from;

You are my defense,
Into Your arms I run;

All my faith, all my dreams
Whether I fail, or whether I succeed

You're teaching Your child,
Your voice I hear;

Though You're way beyond the stars,
I still feel You near.

Verse 2:

When I'm standing in the midst,
Of a powerful storm;

I can look up to You and know,
You're in control;

That's why I have peace,
That's why I can smile, and say;

My Father knows what's best;
For His precious child;

Verse 3:

So when a time in your life,
Has brought you much grief;

You have tried to work it out,
But you can find no relief;

Remember God's in control,
And He is your Source;

There's purpose in the pain,
Give it to the Lord;
He's teaching you,
And showing His grace;

"Hold on my child!"
You will hear Him say;

Let God complete His work,
You'll be better in the end;

For joy comes in the morning,
And you will smile once again!

Introduction

Picture this: You have a room in your home that looks fairly good, but there are scrapes, dents, stains, etc. When people come to visit, these minor flaws are not necessarily noticeable to others. As the owner and resident of the home, you are familiar with every detail of the room and you see the flaws. You envision how much better your home could look if the room was improved.

So you begin the process of remodeling. It starts with an idea of what you want the room to look like. As the creator of that idea, in your mind's eye, only you can visualize what the end result will be once all the remodeling is complete.

To turn your idea into a reality, you hire a carpenter. Here's where the pain begins. A crushing, breaking, tearing, and ripping out must occur. All the old flawed materials must be completely removed. In this state, the room is an eyesore to those who are not privy to the end result. The room has been stripped of everything and already the flaws are absent. You, as the creator of the idea, are excited about the demolished room even in its unfinished state because you can visualize the end result.

Those who did not see the flaws to begin with speculate among themselves that the remodeling must have been the result of an even greater problem. Maybe there was foundation or termite or black mold problems. But others who have experienced remodeling in their own homes catch the vision of your plan. They know how this process works and though they cannot see the finished room, they know the end result will be impressive.

After all the hard work has been done and the temporary displacement has been endured, the reward comes. Now there is restoration. The room is clean, beautiful, shiny, and without stains. Not only has your plan been fulfilled in that room, now others can see that there was a purpose for the temporary pain. The room is so much better than before.

Now it can serve multiple purposes. It accommodates everyone quite nicely now. You can sit back and relax, knowing that the task is over. The work has been done. The purpose has been fulfilled. Now you have a room that's better than before!

To understand that there is purpose in our pain, we must first understand that God will receive glory in all circumstances, the good times and the bad times. He doesn't necessarily receive glory during our pain, but He will receive glory as a result of it.

Let's relate this story to our own lives. God is the owner/resident and you are the home (in Biblical terms, the temple). He sees how a remodeling/improvement is necessary. He allows for the demolition because He needs the flawed materials of your life removed. But in His infinite wisdom, He knows just how much to strip away without causing permanent damage.

In the midst of this process, others may begin to speculate on reasons for your pain. They may say your foundation in Christ is not stable; that you have allowed sin to creep in (termites); or that you had deep hidden addictions (black mold).

But those who have personally experienced God's re-modeling process understand that God has a master plan. After the flaws are removed, He then restores so that His glory can shine before men. He fashions your temple into a work of greater service for advancing His kingdom. The end result . . . God's temple is more useful than it was before.

My objective in writing this book is two-fold: 1) To share a miracle story of the birth of the House of Disciples, a great ministry; and, 2) To share how God's sovereign hand was working through every detail, every triumph and every pain to make us all greater servants for Him.

Every believer in Christ suffers pain. The Bible teaches this in I Cor. 10:13. Trials, tests and temptations are "common to all man." But the internal struggle begins when we cannot identify what the pain is for. I know, I've been there. I wrestled with many ideologies presented to me while growing up in this faith walk.

But the belief that haunted me the most was the one questioning God's supreme reign. No matter what life threw at me, I could not conclude within my heart that God was hands-off, leaving me to fend for myself while under distress. No one could tell me that this pain was for no avail and without cause. Surely, the Architect of my life was not taken by surprise and twiddling His thumbs wondering what to do next. That is not the God we serve.

This book is aimed toward confronting unbelief and trust in God. This book tells the story of struggles in my personal walk with the Lord and the life of House of Disciples. Throughout this book, I'm going to relate pain to purpose, while sharing an inspiring story of God's unrelenting faithfulness.

Chapter One
Broken For Greatness

"I have had it! Enough is enough and I will tolerate this nonsense no longer!" I yelled, while kneeling beside my bed. "God, you have got to do something! I can't take this any longer." At the same time I'm crying and hollering out to God, I have a fistful of my hair, about to pull what little I have left, all the way out of my scalp. I was so upset that my face felt like it was on fire.

I was on staff at a church in Virginia and I was working for a pastor, who I believed to be a dictator. No matter what I did, it wasn't good enough. No matter how hard I tried, my effort always came up short from his perspective. After two years of this, I knew something had to give. I felt like a ruler bending and bending, about to snap in two.

The events leading up to that moment started one morning as I waited for the pastor to arrive at the office. I walked in without knocking or getting permission from his secretary.

I said sternly, "We need to talk."

I sat across from his desk on the edge of the chair and poured my heart out about what all was going wrong. I told him that he should just let me do my job and stay out of it. I did not need him following me around, watching my every move and always telling me where to turn, when to turn and how to turn.

"What did you hire me for if you were planning on doing my job for me?" I asked. With my chest puffed out and eyebrows still squinted together, I sat back in the chair and waited for a cannonball of words to come back at me...how correct I was in my assumption.

With obvious bewilderment, he started off by saying, "I have never had a staff member speak to me this way."

There's an 'ole saying: "People don't remember what you say as much as how you make them feel." I don't remember from that moment on what all was said or how long I was in his office, but I totally recount how I felt overwhelmed with frustration, hurt and anger.

So here I am, beside my bed crying out to God about how I have been so mistreated. My Bible was on my night stand. I picked it up and dropped it on my bed. I didn't know where to turn but, out of desperation, I knew I needed to read and pray for some answers. I started to read where it had opened and the first words my eyes laid sight on was Isaiah 58:9 "...if you do away with the yoke from your midst, with the pointing finger and malicious talk."

I needed to read no further. I knew at that moment that the stress and heartache I had been facing was a result of my own doing. Pride and anger had taken a strong hold in my life and I was too busy pointing the finger at everyone else to realize it.

Six hours later I picked myself up off the floor from praying, repenting and studying the whole chapter thoroughly. I was truly changed. I had been broken. God had used this whole situation for my good. He was bringing me to this place where I would stop, take a self inventory of my own actions and identify the character flaws in my life.

I walked into my home office, turned on my computer and started typing the pastor an email: "I cannot tell you how sorry I am for my actions. All you ever tried to do was help and reach me. I was the one pushing you away and taking everything you did the wrong way. Please forgive me. Why you did not fire me on the spot, I'll never know, but thank you for everything."

After that breakthrough, my days were much different. I had peace. I entered into a time of rest in the Lord. I had taken responsibility for my actions and it felt great!

Don't Touch My Bone
(Result of Our Own Sin)

I saw this video that was circulating around. The name of the video was, "Don't Touch My Bone." It was hilarious. The video was about a dog, sitting in a lounge chair, gnawing on a bone. He began to growl and snarl at his own back leg that started creeping closer to his bone. He continued to growl until his back leg moved away. Each time his foot crept close again, he would begin to growl and snarl, getting more agitated each time it happened. He became so upset that he even bit his own foot. It seemed he never once realized he was biting his own foot because he did it several times.

It made me realize how true a picture this is of our own lives. Oftentimes we are our own worst enemy. The trials we are facing are a direct result of our own actions. Sin is simply disobedience to God's Word. When we are disobedient to God's Word, there are consequences.

David experienced consequences for his actions when he chose to take Bathsheba as his own wife and have her husband murdered in order to accomplish it. (1 Samuel 11 and 12) David also experienced the consequences of his actions when God gave him a direct order not to number the people of Israel, but he did it anyway. (2 Samuel 24)

I experienced consequences because I was too busy blaming others while biting my own foot. It was God all along trying to get me to look in the mirror.

So here's a question to ponder: Who actually sets the consequence for our actions? Man does not, God does. Although it would appear that man is serving as judge over us, the Word describes the heavens announcing, "God is the judge, and He is always honest."[1]

God may at times use individuals to set the consequences, but God is ultimately the one in control. We should take comfort in knowing that God sets the consequences because He is good, fair, just and a merciful God who knows the secrets of our hearts. Even if the initial outcome might seem harsh and unfair, in time it is guaranteed that if you love the Lord and are called according to His purpose, it will work toward your good.[2]

I can truly appreciate David's comments regarding God's correction after the prophet Gad went to David and made him aware of the consequence for his actions. In II Samuel 24:14, David says, "It's a terrible choice to make! But the Lord is kind, and I'd rather have Him punish us than for anyone else to do it." Knowing that we serve an awesome God who is full of mercy and grace and who knows what is best for us, we should all have that same mindset. It is better to fall into the hands of an angry God than to fall into the hands of men.

---

[1] Psalms 50:6
[2] Romans 8:28

When we make a mistake, some might tell us that we are just reaping what we sowed. Some people separate the process of reaping and sowing from God's attempt to teach and correct us. Some believe that experiencing a difficult time in their life must be because of a previous action.

But the process of reaping and sowing is not a cycle God puts into motion in our lives then turns it loose with no future involvement from Him. No, God Himself, keeps an account of our actions, just as he does our every idle word;[3] just as He keeps an account of every tear we shed; just as He keeps an account of our giving; and just as He keeps an account of our works and talents.

God knows exactly when to award us with His favor for the acts of kindness and servanthood we display throughout our lives. And God knows exactly when to bring back around the mistakes we have made so we will be able to learn from them and know not to do those things again. He also uses our own actions to teach others His ways, to show them their transgressions, and give them the opportunity to escape making the same mistakes.

One thing is for sure, God is not sitting on His throne leaning over ready to smack you on the head every time you make a mistake. This picture some people carry of our Lord is a complete myth. God is in the business of teaching His pupils through His Word and taking the opportunity to teach us through our own actions.

A few musical albums and films give the audience a "behind the scenes" look at how the media were made. It shows meetings by actors, producers and directors. It

---

[3] Matthew 12:36

shows outtakes where the actor got his or her lines mixed up. It shows footage of what all went into making a great film or music album.

Now, we see the great Billy Grahams. We hear of the brave missionaries going into foreign lands to preach the Gospel. But what we don't often see is the behind-the-scenes footage of that minister's life. We don't see what all went into making him or her great.

Just as you never see a director, sitting in his chair in the middle of a film, you don't see the director walking out onto a set interrupting the caption to give input; nor do you hear a producer adding his own ad-libs into an artist's song. No, those guys are responsible for making the actors and artists great, the storyline easy to follow and keeping the intensity and quality high.

Behind the scenes is where God is. He is directing, correcting and positioning us into the best possible place we can be in to make us GREAT!

What happened to me is I was "acting" on my own. I wasn't listening to my director. I was trying to direct my own film. Therefore, He saw the need to interrupt my life. In love, He wanted to teach me some valuable lessons through the process of my own mistakes. And I learned greatly.

Coming Home

Although I was born in Memphis, Tennessee, I was raised in a small town in central Texas called Corsicana. So a few months after God broke me for greater service, I was able to return home. One morning while working at my desk, charting an anthem for my orchestra, the phone rings.

"Hello?" I answered.

"Hey Tim...it's Jonathan. You ready to come on back home to Texas? I need an associate here at the church and God laid you on my heart to call." he said.

Little did Jonathan know that although everything was going fine, I knew that the mission was accomplished there in Virginia. God had sent me there for a season and with a purpose and it was completed.

My family and I arrived in Mesquite, Texas, in January 2003. I was approaching ministry with a new lease on life. The agenda for my life had changed from advancing my kingdom, to sincerely advancing God's. I had compassion for people like never before.

Several weeks passed and I had gotten settled into my role at the church. Yet I knew there was more I was supposed to be doing for Christ. It seemed odd. Here I was in the ministry. Every day I woke up and my job was to minister at a church. One would think that it was a fulfilling service to God. But, I still had emptiness and a void that I knew I needed fulfilled in my calling. I decided I would expand on the gifts God had already given me.

So I placed a phone call to a friend and talked to him about helping me start an outreach team. I wanted to put together a team of musicians to go into areas of our community where the less fortunate lived. We would find a park where we would pass out clothes and food and play music that would proclaim the love of Christ.

Also, during this time songs started coming to me during my devotion time. So I also began researching what it would take to make an album that we could pass out to all the needy people.

I really didn't know what I was doing or where I was

going. All I knew was there was more to be done than what I was doing. In my journal, I found myself writing continually, "God use me more. Maximize the gifts within me. I surrender to you."

Our team was made up of Trey Swain, Dan "the Man" Phillips, Aaron Martin, Sanford Bates, Larry Locker and myself. We named our outreach team Just Faith. We came up with the name because we wanted to declare at every event that all it takes to receive Christ into your heart is Just Faith.

I was excited. This ship was setting sail and I felt I was walking into a greater calling to help more people.

Our first event was at Bachman Lake in North Dallas. I couldn't stop smiling all day. It was a wonderful day of giving and sharing the love of Christ with others. We passed out food and sang until we had no voice left. Over 20 people gave their hearts to the Lord. It was awesome!

I returned to the church and gave a report of everything that God had done. We immediately started planning another outreach. Altogether, we did another 50 that year.

A.K.A. White Chocolate

While in Virginia, my choir was made up of many different cultures. There were Caucasians, African-Americans, some from the Philippines and other countries. Because there was such diversity, I always tried to do a variety of music. I do have to admit one thing though. I like groovy, funky, jazzy music. So I have a tendency to throw in more of those types of songs than any other.

Wednesday evening after a choir rehearsal, I'm standing in front talking to everyone as they are leaving and I noticed that some were saying, "See you Sunday, WC."

I've never claimed to be the sharpest knife in the drawer because it takes me a little longer to catch onto things than others. So not thinking too much about it, I just dismissed it as people being funny.

However, at the next choir rehearsal I began hearing the same thing. I questioned some of the folks and, come to find out, I had been given the nickname White Chocolate or W. C. by Delores Johnson, one of the choir members. Dolores is an African-American who loved black gospel music. So we had that in common. However, what we didn't have in common is that I'm white. So, she would comment to me often, "You're white on the outside, but a whole lotta' chocolate on the inside."

During my time as the choir director, the choir had a lot of fun with me over this nickname. When I moved back to Texas, I thought for sure that nickname had ended. I was wrong. As we began to return to the same areas to do outreaches and started getting to know the people on a personal level, they started referring to us as WC.

Here I go again. It didn't matter that I would stand behind a microphone in front of everyone letting them know that we are an outreach team named Just Faith. It didn't matter that the front of our t-shirts read "Just Faith Outreach." It didn't really matter that I did not want to be called WC. Everywhere we went, it seemed like everyone we met called us White Chocolate.

Finally, I embraced it. I just decided that it's not the name that makes you who you are. Its Christ living through you that makes you who you are. So now our outreach team is called White Chocolate. Got a sweet tooth?

Two Hours of Trust

I served the church in Mesquite for three years. I loved the congregation and the pastor. Our outreach team was taking on a life of its own. More people were getting involved and I felt like I was fulfilling my destiny and calling. Things were going very well.

One day, I got a call from a friend who served at a church in Tyler, Texas. He said that they were preparing for a big event in East Texas with some well-known speakers and artists. He said the event would be televised nationally and wanted to know if I could help musically.

I agreed and began working with the choirs, TV network and others involved in the production. The event was to be held at a large church in Longview, Texas.

I drove down to Longview for the rehearsal and one evening while taking a 10-minute break from rehearsal, one of the pastors from the church approached me. He said that they were currently looking for a music director and wanted to know if I would be interested in submitting a résumé.

I responded without any hesitation, "Oh, no sir. I'm right where I need to be." I told him everything that I had going on in Mesquite and that there was no chance of me leaving. Plus, I had not served as a music director for over three years and really didn't miss it.

After rehearsal, I got into my car for my two-hour drive back home. I was pumped. Rehearsal was excellent and I was thinking this event is going to rock East Texas like never before. I cranked my car, fastened my seat belt and turned on my CD player. As I put the car in reverse, wrapped my arm around the back of the passenger's seat to look back, I heard the Lord say, "Do you trust me?"

I slowly eased my foot off the brake and started backing out, knowing that this was going to be a long two-hour ride home. Christ followers don't hear God with natural ears. We hear the Holy Spirit within us, with our spiritual ears. We don't walk by sight, we walk by faith. I had heard that voice before. I recognized the tugging in my heart and the soft, gentle whisper.

I began pulling out of the parking lot, and then responded, "Yes. I trust You."

"I want you to move to Longview," He said.

"But God, everything is going so well for us in Mesquite. We are touching lives for You. You don't want all that to end, do you? Who will take my place? How can they do it without me?" I responded.

God asked me again, "Do you trust me?"

I tried every excuse I could muster up to try to change God's mind… like that was going to happen. I knew what I had to do. A month later, I was living in Longview serving on staff at the church as the music director.

Nowhere to Look but Up

Within a few weeks of being in Longview, the life I had was beginning to crumble. My marriage began to get severely strained. My wife had just graduated from college and taken a job she loved in Dallas before we moved to Longview. She was driving back and forth from Dallas. I was exhausted from trying to make all the outreaches and take care of my responsibilities at the church. My travels were keeping me away from home. I was neglecting my family and was very tired. I was spiritually drained and was falling into a pit fast.

I remember the night she left me and the boys. She had decided to move back to Dallas. Our boys, Silas, six, and Malachi, four, at the time were confused and did not understand what was happening.

We helped her pack up all her belongings and put them in the back of her car. The boys gave her a hug goodbye and, as she drove off, I stood in the front yard with each boy under each arm. We watched her drive off, then turned and walked back into the house.

As we sat on the couch in our living room, I had Malachi on my lap and Silas was lying on the floor in front of me. Nothing was said between us. I did not know what to say. I didn't know whether to be strong or let my tears begin to roll. I didn't know whether to try and lighten the mood with daddy being funny or to say nothing at all.

Then Silas broke the silence by asking, "Daddy, is momma coming back home?"

I didn't know what to tell him. So I just said, "I don't know, baby."

He asked again, "Daddy, when will we see momma again? Is she coming back home?"

This time I thought I would share what I truly believed instead of avoiding it. "Baby, I don't think she is coming back."

I've always taught my kids that God answers prayer. I remember while they were growing up that we would pray for our dogs, cats or anything else if the boys thought they were sick. But I didn't realize what kind of impact it made on the kids until Silas's next comment. "But daddy I prayed that momma would come back and you said that God answers my prayers."

I could not hold my tears any longer. I pulled him up into my lap as all three of us began to cry. I had Silas on my left and Malachi on my right. I pulled them close to me and leaned back on the couch. About 2 o'clock in the morning I woke up. We had cried ourselves to sleep. I got up, put the boys in their beds and went to my room to pray.

I had nowhere to look but up. I had lost my marriage. I had lost my outreach ministry. I just knew I was going to be fired from the church. I was at the bottom of a deep pit.

Chapter Two
Permission Granted

I grew up most of my life believing that Satan could work his evil and manipulate my life at his own free will. I believed that at any point in my life I could be facing an assault on my family, ministry, church and all other areas of my life. I thought Satan could operate inside of God's borders of protection. I further believed that Satan's power over this earth, as a result of Adam's sin, now made me subject to him and I had to tolerate this devil.

But through this tragedy in my life, I began to study God's word and spend more time in prayer. During this time, God gave me a revelation. He revealed to me that my thinking regarding Satan and his power was all wrong. Jesus came to destroy the works of Satan.[4]

He told His disciples, "These things I have spoken to you, that in me you might have peace. In the world you will have tribulation; but be of good cheer; for I have <u>overcome the world</u>."[5] [6]

God showed me that the devil cannot attack any part of my life, unless His permission is granted. He showed me that He is a loving and caring Father who is willing

---

[4] I John 3:8
[5] Emphasis added
[6] John 16:33

to allow His children to face difficult times in their lives so that He can reveal more of Himself to us. In turn, we will reveal more of ourselves to Him.

"Allowed"

After receiving this revelation from the Lord, I got so excited that I wanted to share it with everyone. I went to my pastor and asked him if I could teach on this subject during one of our Wednesday evening services. He granted permission but warned me that I was about to teach on something that could be very controversial. He encouraged me to stand upon what God had revealed to me but to be prepared to face some hard questions after the teaching.

To be honest, I thought he was being overly sensitive. I left his office thinking to myself, "How could anyone not see it this way? It is very plain in the scriptures. Surely God has given this to me so that everyone can be blessed." How wrong I was!

I did face some hard questions and they all revolved around the word "allowed." What I learned was that people who face difficult times in their lives have a hard time seeing God. But He is in hardships because there is nothing that you will ever face in life that your sovereign God did not allow to happen.

The Bible says, "You are tempted in the same way that everyone else is tempted. But God can be trusted not to <u>allow</u>[7] you to be tempted too much, and He will show you how to escape from your temptations."[8] The key in the passage is the word "allow."

---

[7] Emphasis Added
[8] 1 Corinthians 10:13

Let's take a look at the life of Joseph in the latter chapters of Genesis. This story is an example of how the Lord allowed three major tragedies to happen to Joseph. At the end of these trials, however, Joseph understood what God had done in his life. And he even declared that God had allowed all the things to happen to him for a greater purpose.[9]

Joseph was born to Jacob (Jacob's name was later changed by God to Israel) and he was a model boy.[10] At the age of 17, God gave Joseph two dreams.[11] These dreams were powerful and told of things to come in his life. But his brothers and even his father Jacob did not receive the dreams. Jacob rebuked his son over the second dream and it made his brothers turn against him even more.

It is important to note that Joseph was excited about what God had showed him through the dreams. He could not wait to let everyone know that God had big plans for his life. I'm sure Joseph was very eager for the fulfillment of those dreams. He probably lay awake a few nights just fantasizing and playing out in his own mind what kind of a ruler he would become.

You would have similar feelings if this should happen to you as well. If a word from God has been spoken over you or revealed to you through some other means, you would more than likely experience great excitement. It is exciting to know that God has great plans for His people.

Right after God gave Joseph the dreams, Jacob sent him to check on his brothers and take them some items

[9] Genesis 45: 5-7
[10] Genesis 37
[11] Genesis 37: 5-11

while they were out working in the fields. When he arrived, the first tragedy occurs. His own brothers plot to kill him. They cast him into a pit and then sell him into slavery. They put blood on his cloak and bring it to his father and tell him that Joseph is dead so he would not go looking for him.

I'm sure at this point Joseph is saying, "Why God? What happened to the dreams you gave me? Has the devil stolen my victory? Did Satan just rob me of my destiny?" Let's continue exploring this story.

Joseph is now a slave in Egypt.[12] He is no longer in control of his life – but God is! Joseph was bought as a slave and was now serving a man named Potiphar. Potiphar was the captain of the guard in Egypt. He was one of the officers of Pharaoh. He held a high position in that country.

Is it by chance that Joseph ended up at a high ranking officer's home instead of in the home of a common Egyptian working man, just trying to make ends meet? I think not! Joseph needed to learn from the best. He needed to learn how to conduct business and manage many people because he would use that knowledge later on. I believe God sent him to Potiphar so he could learn from a man who had vast experience.

Notice one more example of God's goodness. The Bible says that the "Lord was with him."[13] God is with you, too, during your hardships. God is directly involved in your life during your painful experiences. Let's continue exploring this story.

Now let's look at the second tragedy. Joseph rejects

---

[12] Genesis 39
[13] Genesis 39:2

the advances of Potiphar's wife because he wants to keep his integrity with God and with Potiphar by not sleeping with her. Potiphar, however, believes his wife's lies regarding Joseph and subsequently throws Joseph into the king's prison. Things are getting worse.

Now Joseph is a slave, in prison, in a foreign country. I'm sure while sitting in that jail cell he reflected back to the dreams God gave him and said to himself "Everything seems out of control. Can God not find me? Did He lose track of me somehow? What is going on?"

But notice what prison he is in – the King's prison. This is Pharaoh's personal prison for the prisoners he personally wants bound. Joseph was not with the general population of prisoners.

Is it by chance that he ended up at the King's personal prison? I think not! God was setting things up for Joseph and placing him in the exact location that was necessary for him to be later noticed by the king. And once again, look at how God is with Joseph right in the middle of his crisis just as God is with us during our times of crisis. Let's continue exploring this story.

The king's butler and baker had offended the king[14] so Pharaoh cast them into his prison. While in prison, they both had dreams. The dreams they had troubled them because they knew there was a meaning to them. But they thought there was no one in prison to interpret the dreams for them (or so they thought).

Well, along comes Joseph. One might think that the last thing Joseph would want to hear about was another dream. But Joseph was keeping his faith in God. He interprets the dreams for the men and everything came to pass exactly as he had told them it would. Joseph only

---

[14] Genesis 40

had one request for the butler: "Please remember me and help me get out of here."

Then the third tragedy occurs. The butler forgets about Joseph and the interpretation of the dreams as well as the care and concern Joseph had shown him.

Have you ever helped someone in their time of need and when you needed an act of kindness, they couldn't stop thinking of themselves long enough to lend a hand? I'm sure Joseph saw the good he had done for the butler as a "get out of jail free" card.

But those hopes soon turned to despair as the days grew longer and longer. The walls seemed to close in on him as he realized that he had been forgotten. It could have very well crossed his mind that there went his last chance for freedom. I'm sure he looked up to God at some point and said, "What more can I do Lord? I'm trying as hard as I can to do right before you. Please, please, please help!"

But God works His will according to His plan and in His timing. And as the song says: "He's an on time God, yes He is. He may not come when you want it, but He'll be there right on time."

Another dream now comes into the story, but this time it was the King himself who had it.[15] The king calls all his wise men together, but no one can find the meaning of the dream.

At that point, the butler remembers Joseph! The king calls for Joseph to be brought to him from prison. Joseph interprets the dreams and because of this, Pharaoh makes him second in command, right under the king himself. Joseph goes from prisoner to ruler in a matter of a few minutes.

---

[15] Genesis 41

Now why did God allow all of that to happen to Joseph? Why was it even necessary for him to go through all of that? Was there not an easier way? The answer is – no. God was about to bring a seven-year famine to the land. God was not about to break the promises he had made to Joseph. With Joseph now ruler over the land, he was in a position to help his father Jacob during this famine and he did help him. All the training (trials) Joseph went through helped prepare him for his destiny.

We cannot see what God sees – the future. God is accomplishing a greater work in our lives that will even affect others. It is not just your life that is at stake. God is considering everyone around you when He allows trials to come your way.

We serve a God who is in complete control. "For I know the plans I have for you, says the Lord. They are plans for good and not for disaster, to give you a future and a hope."[16]   God desires the best for you and from you. He has a plan and a purpose for your life. His plans are for you to live productively. He has no desire for you to end this life in disaster by spending eternity in hell. But His plans will not be fulfilled if we do not give Him lordship over our lives. And these plans will not be fulfilled if we do not acknowledge Him, even in our troubled times.

How do we know for sure that God allows hardships to come on the path to our destiny? Let's take a look at Job and Peter. God gave permission to the devil to test their faith and relationship with God.

Let's consider Job. God asks Satan if he had considered His servant Job for testing. Notice what Satan's

---

[16] Jeremiah 29:11 (NLT)

response is: "Have not You made a hedge about him, and about his house, and about all that he has on every side? You have blessed the works of his hands, and his substance is increased in the land."[17]

What Satan was actually saying was, "Hey God, there is nothing I can do to him without your permission. You have a hedge of protection around him, his family and his belongings."

But God gives Satan permission to only operate within the borders God has given him. "And the Lord said unto Satan, 'Behold, all that he has is in your power; only upon himself put not forth your hand'."[18] God is in control. Not Satan! God allowed Satan to attack Job, but with conditions.

Even Job, who experienced such horrible tragedies one right after another, understood that God must be acknowledged in all things. After losing all and being pressured by his wife to curse God and die, Job's reply was simply this: "Should we accept only good things from the hand of God and never anything bad?"[19] Job had lost everything, including his health, yet he acknowledged God in his pain. He knew God had allowed the tragedies for a reason, even if he could not see the reasons at that moment in time.

Now let's look at how God allowed the testing of Simon Peter the night Jesus was betrayed. The setting: Jesus and his disciples are taking Communion. Jesus turns to Simon Peter and addresses him in an informal way: "Simon, Simon. Behold, Satan has desired to have you; that he may sift you as wheat; but I have prayed for you,

---

[17] Job 1:10
[18] Job 1:12
[19] Job 2:10

that your faith fail not; and when you are converted, strengthen the brothers."[20]

How did Jesus know this? It is obvious that during one of Jesus' times of getting away to pray to His Father, God revealed to Jesus that Satan was asking to attack Peter. Jesus then prays to God on Peter's behalf. Pay close attention to the prayer that Jesus prayed. He did not ask God to deliver Peter from the attack. He did not pray for God to smite Satan for even asking. Instead, Jesus knew there were some things in Peter's life that needed to be addressed, so Jesus prayed for Peter's faith.

We can see that there was probably the issue of pride in Peter's life by the way he responded to Jesus: "I am ready to go with You, both unto prison and unto death!"[21]

Jesus knew that a sifting was exactly what was needed to take place in Peter's life to expose to Peter, himself, the imperfections that existed within. So God lifted His hedge of protection over Peter's life and allowed him to be tested by Satan.

Let's take a closer look at another word Jesus used in this passage – "converted."

Peter believed in Jesus as "the Christ, the Son of the living God."[22] The use of the word was not referring to Peter being converted to Christianity. So what did Jesus mean when He spoke to Peter of his conversion?

The word "converted" is *epistrepho* in the Greek and it means: "to return, to revert, come again." Somewhere along the way, while following Jesus, Peter had allowed some character flaws to enter into his heart. Peter needed to go through a time of sifting so these flaws

[20] Luke 22: 31-32
[21] Luke 22:33
[22] Matthew 16:16

could be addressed by God while Peter was in his most broken state.

Now what did Jesus say would happen after Peter was converted? He said that Peter would strengthen his brothers. God had big plans for Peter's life. God knew that with the flaws Peter had, God could not accomplish the greatness He had in store for him. It is very possible that God saw that Peter couldn't stand before the thousands and call them unto Jesus. It is very possible that God knew Peter could not have received the anointing to heal the sick with only his shadow if He had allowed him to continue to carry pride and other flaws within himself.

Now consider your own life. More than likely, you are reading this because you are walking through a difficult time. So what should you do when out of the clear blue you suddenly find yourself in the middle of a trial? What reaction should you have when in an unexpected moment? Or what if you experience a knee-buckling tragedy? How can you make it through this crisis?

When You Are Being Attacked, Wave the White Flag!

The answer is: When you find yourself being attacked by the enemy of your soul, wave the white flag of surrender unto God. And when you are being attacked by the devil, understand that there is purpose in the attack. When a loved one dies without warning, there is purpose in your hurt. And when your child is experiencing an illness, look to the Lord as the source of your help. When your employer has just informed you that the company is moving in a different direction and you are not included in the move, understand that God is accomplishing a good work, and know that there is purpose in the pain you are experiencing.

In some of the churches my family attended when I was a young boy, I was taught to always address the devil when under attack. I was told that I was in a "war against the devil" and I must "learn to fight!" Phrases like, "I bind you Satan over this city, country, world, universe, galaxy . . ." were commonly used in many of the church services I attended. I was taught to blame everything on the devil, believing that every bad thing or tragedy that happened was directly caused by him. Although it is true Satan is the one causing these bad things to happen, we need to realize that he is only able to do so with God's permission.

Please don't misunderstand me. I believe that we must take our rightful place against the "wiles of the devil,"[23] but we must learn first to turn our focus from Satan and the tragedy and re-focus on God and what He is trying to accomplish in our lives through these tragedies. In order to do that, I believe the first action that must be taken is total submission to God.

"Submit yourself therefore unto God, resist the devil and he will flee from you."[24] I'm convinced that the order in which James wrote this verse is just as important as the action itself. When faced with a mountain of despair, we must first submit and surrender our lives to God. Next, we must put on the armor of God, which allows us to stand against Satan. Once we have been obedient to the Word of the Lord and have done what God has asked us to do, God will rebuke Satan and command

---

[23] Ephesians 6:11
[24] James 4:7

him to flee from us.

I believe too many Christians today get the order backward. They immediately address the devil and focus on him instead of focusing on God. They try binding, loosing, stomping and kicking the devil without first seeking God and finding out why the devil is there in the first place. Satan is never involved in your affairs unless God has permitted him to be there.

The scripture, "Whatsoever you bind on earth, will be bound in heaven; and whatsoever you loose on earth, will be loosed in heaven"[25] is referring to the authority Jesus has given to us over the devil. But what if the devil is there because it's God's choice? That appears to have been what happened in the Job and Peter scenarios. They could have tried binding the devil all day long, but the devil was there with the permission of God.

So what if God has allowed the devil to mess with an area of your life? What if God is trying to work something out in your life that is hindering Him from accomplishing His perfect will? What if all you ever do is keep trying to bind the devil and never address God or ask Him what He is up to? If all you ever do is address the devil and do not first submit to God, then you will never learn what it is God is trying to teach you. You will continue to go through the same trial over and over again until you finally pause and "look unto the hills from whence comes your help"[26] and allow God to perform the operation inside your heart that is needed.

The apostle James states, ". . . you have not because you ask not. You ask, and receive not, because you ask amiss, that you may consume it upon your own

---

[25] Matthew 18:18
[26] Psalms 121

desires."[27] Everything must be asked in accordance with God's will, even when you are binding the devil against the temptation you are facing. "If it is your will God," should end your every prayer.

Victim or Victorious?

After teaching on this subject one afternoon, a man approached me with the question, "If God is allowing me to face my situation, then what need do I have for any faith?"

I shared with the gentleman, "Faith is called upon, demanded and is required more than ever when you know God is allowing your pain, unless you are just thinking of yourself as a victim of life's challenges or the devil's torment."

There are two ways we can view our painful trials: 1) We can have faith and trust in God and know that He is in control of everything and has allowed them for a purpose and for our good. This attitude places your faith, life and pain in His hands. Or, 2) You can consider yourself a victim of the devil or life in general (however you might perceive it). And you can go through life being knocked around and bruised up, with your head hanging low. You might say, "Well, I guess the devil decided to pick on me today. I must be doing something right."

No! No! No! You are not a victim! You are victorious through Jesus! You are a child of the Most High God. You have a heavenly Father that loves you! He is interested personally in each and every small detail of your everyday life. That is why you are going through the

---
[27] James 4:2

pain. That is why you need to have great faith and trust in the Lord. Faith in Him who created you and is emptying you. He is pouring Himself into you.

It is in your most broken state that God does the greatest work. There will always be pain after an operation, but you have a surgeon who will not make a mistake. He will not cut too deep. He will not leave you all alone. He will be right there with you while you are healing. "He will never leave you nor forsake you."[28]

Faith means to trust in something or someone when there is no proof it exists. "Faith is the substance of things hoped for, the evidence of things not seen."[29] So how does faith apply in your everyday walk with the Lord? First, you have to have faith and believe on Jesus as the Christ and the Redeemer of your soul. Secondly, you have to have faith/trust in God and surrender your life to Him. It takes a lot of faith/trust to give God your everything.

Let's look at the story of Abraham and Isaac in Genesis 22, for instance. God himself (not the devil) spoke to Abraham to test him. What was God testing? He was testing Abraham's faith/trust and surrender to God.

God does not want anything or anybody to come before Him in your life. God asks Abraham to sacrifice his son Isaac. He was not just any son but the son that Abraham and Sarah had waited for so long. But Abraham was obedient.

I can imagine the scene. Isaac looks around for the animal that's to be presented to God. He points out a few on the way. "There's one, Dad. Did you see that one? Let's go get him."

---

[28] Hebrews 13:5
[29] Hebrews 11:1

But Abraham just keeps walking in silence, never answering. When they reach the appointed place, all of a sudden his father takes him by the arm, looks directly into his eyes and says, "Son, I'm sorry, but you are the sacrifice I must make to the Lord." Both Abraham and Isaac cry deeply. Isaac, totally innocent, lies there shaking in fear. He is wondering why his daddy, the one that should be protecting him from harm, is now about to do him harm. He is wondering why God would want to do this to him. Maybe he even blamed himself.

Abraham, very downcast in his heart, tries to keep his faith in God. But he truly loves this precious gift of a beautiful boy God has given him. He looks up to heaven with one last glance, as if silently to ask for this cup to pass from him. Trusting in the Lord, and with what little energy he could muster, he stretches forth his hand with the knife in it and . . . "Abraham! Abraham!" Once again, God shows up right on time. An angel stops him, God provides a ram for the sacrifice, and Abraham passes the test. All he had, he gave to the Lord. What a beautiful story of trust in God.

The more you trust God, the more control He will have. Those areas you keep to yourself and insist on reigning over and dictating their every action, those are the areas God does not carry in His hands. You will ultimately fail without His involvement.

If you need a healing in your body, trust and pray to Jesus, who took 39 stripes across His back and shed His blood for the healing of our bodies.

In His timing and according to His will, not yours, things will be accomplished so that He can receive the glory. If you are in need of a financial breakthrough, trust and pray to God who owns the "cattle of a thousand hills."[30] And in His timing and according to His will, not ours, it will be accomplished so that He can receive the glory.

If your marriage is broken and in need of repair, trust and pray to God who established the "greatest Covenant with all man."[31] And in His timing and according to His will, not yours, it will be accomplished so that He can receive the glory.

"Seek first, the Kingdom of God, and His righteousness; and all these things will be added unto you."[32] You seek God first and place your trust and faith in Him, and He will take care of the needs in your life. It's your job to do the seeking. It's His job to do the adding.

Have faith/trust in the Lord enough to surrender your all (health, children, finances . . . everything and everybody) to Him. Then you will not be a victim, but a victorious believer who knows without a doubt that you are in the hands of the Almighty!

---

[30] Psalms 50:10
[31] Hebrews 8:6
[32] Matthew 6:33

Chapter Three
Restored Through Healing

The church offered me a leave of absence and assured me that they would walk through this valley with me. I was amazed. The whole congregation embraced my family and extended grace like I have never seen or personally experienced before. This was the church of God operating at its best. I spent the next two years healing and being restored.

God sent a beautiful and most caring woman named Misty into my life. She had gone through the same experience in her previous marriage and could relate to all the emotions and struggles. We married after courting and dating for almost a year. Misty is a prime example of Romans 8:28 "...works all things out for our good." Losing my marriage was the most hurtful event of my life. There were moments when I felt all hope was lost. But looking back now, God orchestrated everything for my good.

Surely Goodness and Mercy

When we face trying times, it is critical for us to understand who God truly is. It is necessary for us to identify His sovereignty and His goodness. It is when we are going through a family crisis, or about to lose a loved one, or having difficulty with a son or daughter that we must be willing to accept the fact that God is in complete control. And that He loves you with a Father's unconditional love. When dealing with sensitive subjects, such as tragedies that happen in our lives, severe circumstances and hardships, we must know intimately who it is that we serve. We must understand more clearly the attributes of our Abba Father.

Hardships cause different individuals to react in different ways. For me, hardship produced a desire to learn more about the Lord. To be honest with you, I wanted to know just exactly what He was doing up there because I had hit rock bottom.

Early on in my ministry, my brother was charged with a very serious crime. Up to that point in life, through my family's influence and my parents' wealth, there was no mess we couldn't get ourselves out of. Well, that all changed!

I remember while the trial was taking place, I was living in another town about three hours away from home and where my brother and parents lived. I would call my parents often to see how everything was going, but I carried a quiet confidence that God was going to "show up" and "show out!" In my immaturity, I just knew God would once again deliver my brother from this. I should have seen the yellow lights all around, warning me, but I chose to ignore them.

Even my own brother called me a couple of times during his week-long trial saying, "Tim, you should come down and see me because things are not going well." But my faith was in what God could do, rather than in who God is.

I was sitting in my office at the church about to walk

out and lead choir rehearsal. I had a couple of awesome songs picked out. My choir was growing and I had some new soloists that could sing until the rafters would shake. Then the phone rang. It was Dad,

"Hey Dad, how are you doing?" I said.

"Hang on a minute," Dad said with his voice very weak and quivering.

"Dad, are you there? What's wrong?"

I heard him barely say, "Please, just give me a minute." A minute or so passed, but it seemed like hours. "He got 55 years," he finally said.

No words can describe the deep feeling of pain, confusion and hurt. It was after 7 p. m. and people were waiting on me. I had to get to choir rehearsal, after all, it was my job. I walked in through the side door. I stood before my choir with tears rolling down my face. All I can say in that moment was, "I need prayer."

It is times like these where the goodness of God escapes us. Our minds are flooded with, "WHY GOD?!" "Why would you let this happen?" "God, you could have prevented this. You could have intervened!"

We know there is no one stronger and more powerful than God. We sat in the Sunday school classes learning of God hardening Pharaoh's heart. We read in Romans that God has the final say.

But as you hunger to know more about our God, He will reveal Himself to you in a greater way.

Jesus is on the mount teaching. In one of the many promises He gives us during this sermon is a promise that if we "hunger and thirst for righteousness,"[33] we are blessed and will be filled. Hunger is an idiom for a strong desire. Who is righteous within us? Jesus is right-

---

[33] Matthew 5:6

eous within us. And what will you be filled with? You will be filled with Jesus, our righteousness. In other words, the more you allow self to decrease, the more He will increase in you. Less of you produces more of Him. God wants a greater intimacy with His children. Pray this, "Lord, empty me!"

Sovereign God

There are many synonyms for God but the one I want to deal with is "Lord." Lord is found 600 times in the New Testament. The word "Lord" in Greek is *Kurios* which means supreme authority, sovereignty. To say that God is sovereign is to declare that God *is* God.

Nebuchadnezzar experienced the sovereignty of God after allowing pride to creep into his heart and subsequently rejecting the advice given by Daniel. This is the only story in the Bible where God supernaturally changed an individual's sanity. He was mentally changed from man to beast. "Nebuchadnezzar did eat grass as an oxen. His body was wet with the dew of heaven, until his hairs were grown like eagle's feathers and his nails like bird's claws."[34] He remained in this state for seven years.

Nebuchadnezzar's judgment from God was actually a very rare mental disease. It is called lycanthropy, which comes from the Greek word *lukos,* meaning a wolf, animal, and *anthropos*, a man, because the person imagines himself to be a wolf, a bear, or some other animal.

At the expiration of the seven years, Nebuchadnezzar was suddenly restored to sanity and began blessing the God of Heaven for His mercy. Notice how he describes

---

[34] Daniel 4:28-35

our Sovereign God: "All the inhabitants of the earth are reputed as nothing; He does according to His will in the army of heaven and among the inhabitants of the earth. No one can restrain His hand or say to Him, 'What have You done?'"[35]

That shows a man who has truly experienced and now understands the sovereign hand of God.

David describes God in this way: "To say that God is sovereign is to declare that He is the Almighty, the Possessor of all power in heaven and earth, so that none can defeat His counsels, thwart His purpose, or resist His will."[36]

To say that God is sovereign is to declare that He is "the Governor among the nations,"[37]; "setting up kingdoms, overthrowing empires, and determining the course of dynasties according to His own good counsel."[38] Paul describes the sovereignty of God as the "only Potentate, the King of kings and the Lord of lords."[39] "Thine, O Lord, is the greatness, and the power, and the glory, and the victory, and the majesty: for all that is in the heaven and in the earth is Thine; Thine is the kingdom, O Lord, and Thou art exalted as Head above all."[40]

Paul further states: "Let every soul be subject unto the higher powers. For there is no power but of God; the powers that be are ordained of God."[41] Presidents, queens, kings, and rulers all are ordained by God.

---

[35] Daniel 4:35
[36] Psalms 115:3
[37] Psalms 22:28
[38] Ephesians 1:11
[39] 1 Timothy 6:15
[40] 1 Chronicles 29:11
[41] Romans 13:1

Paul, the author of Ephesians, Timothy and Romans; David the author of Psalms; and Isaiah and Ezra, authors of the Chronicles; all had a close individual relationship with God. If they knew Him in this way and described His character as being in total control, then why should we consider Him any differently?

By now, you should have an understanding, through scripture, that God is in complete control. The glorious assurance that we have in God's sovereignty is that He can always be depended upon to act justly in everything He does. This occurs not only because He is Sovereign, but He is also Good.

The Goodness of God

Because both Christians and non-Christians alike can quote John 3:16 verbatim, it would seem, because of its familiarity to everyone, that it has lost some of its inspiration. I believe it is still the greatest written demonstration of God's *agape* love for His people: "For God so loved the world that He gave His only begotten Son, that whosoever believeth in Him should not perish but have everlasting life."

Sending His son Jesus to die on a cross was the greatest sacrifice God could have made and He did it for you and me. God is good!

God is love! "Beloved, let us love one another; for love is of God; and everyone that loves is born of God, and knows God. He that loves not, knows not God; for God is love."[42][43] God created love. God is the perfection of love. God is the faultless example of love. Love is not

---

[42] Emphasis Added
[43] I John 4: 7-8

what God does, love is who He is! Through Jesus, God gave the greatest expression of love. God's love is infinite for His children. The depths of God's love cannot be described by anyone. When God says, "I love you," just know, He truly loves you!

However, there is a side of love that we don't often talk about. God loves us so much that He is committed to helping us succeed and become the best that we can be. Love is commitment rather than just an emotion. God is committed to helping his people by forgiving us of our sins when we confess them, comforting us, giving us new mercies each morning, and many other blessings.

But God's love also requires correction and guidance. "For whom the Lord loves He corrects; even as a father the son in whom he delights."[44] And this is the side of God that is not too often mentioned by Christians, and understandably so. Correction is not easy, but it is necessary.

I have three wonderful children, Silas, 11, Malachi, 10, and Emmalee, seven. These kids are wonderful gifts God has given to me. I love them and I would do anything within my means to make them happy. I have spent so much money on them buying toys and games for their entertainment. I participate in their school functions, soccer games, basketball, and all their other activities. I also help them with their homework. We wrestle on the floor, play tag, and watch kids' movies together. We have a lot of fun and spend good quality time with each other.

But I would be doing them an injustice if my only involvement in their lives was just fun and games. As their

---

[44] Proverbs 3:12

father, I am directed by God to show my commitment to them in love. When they are in need of correction and discipline I, as their father, must render it. Solomon wrote: "If I spare correcting my child, then I hate him."[45] Now that's a strong statement. Our heavenly Father would be doing us an injustice if during the times when we need guidance and correction in our lives, He is absent.

We must understand that God is so good and that He loves us so much, that He is willing to be involved in every part of our lives. Sometimes His involvement even requires us to experience testing and trials in order to expose our weaknesses. At times it requires allowing us to follow through with bad choices where He sets the consequences and, as a result, teaches us valuable lessons.

Other times it requires us to experience an unsettling in our surroundings that we eventually recognize as His guidance and direction in our lives. Sometimes His involvement requires us to experience pain. Often these painful experiences are for the purpose of future testimonies. But there is one thing that you can always count on: When you serve a Sovereign God who is in complete control, who loves you unconditionally, and who is looking out for your best interest, He also knows exactly what to bring about in your life to make you a greater servant for Him.

---

[45] Proverbs 13:24

Chapter Four
On The Road Again

Proverbs 3:4 teaches us, "...if you will acknowledge God in all your ways, He will direct your path." Although there are times when it feels like God is a million miles away, we as believers don't live by how we feel, but what we know. Even in the toughest times, I have tried hard to acknowledge God in all my ways. Therefore, I believe He is ordering my steps and directing my path.

After a couple years of restoration, I began travelling down the road of doing outreaches again. But this time was much different for I had learned some valuable lessons about keeping my priorities in alignment-relationship with God, family, then ministry. And this time I had a partner, Misty, who wanted to be involved in the ministry. We feel that we are teammates in this race we run for Christ.

In September 2007, during one of my morning devotions, God led me to Luke 5:4, "Launch out into the deep and let down your nets for a catch." Once again I had heard that still small voice inside me. I didn't fully understand what was about to happen at the time, but I was excited to know that God was going to use me. I typed up an email to our outreach team. I shared that I didn't fully know what this meant, but we needed to start preparing ourselves for a great catch.

In May 2008, we organized a Memorial Day outreach at Maria Luna Park in downtown Dallas with my good friend Larry Locker. At the end of a tremendous day of sharing the love of Christ, Larry did something he had never done before in the seven years I had been ministering alongside him. He called my team forward and asked if he could pray for us.

I could tell when he started that this was not just a prayer of blessing, but this was a prayer of release. He asked God to direct our steps into new open doors. His prayer was as if he sent us out on a new journey. On the way home, we all knew we were released to start doing things locally instead of driving long distances for outreach. And I knew personally that God wanted these same outreaches done in Longview.

I immediately began planning an event in Longview. We decided to name it "Party in the Park." On July 12, 2008, we launched out and organized our own outreach. At the advice of other people, we scheduled it at Birdie Park. The problem was, when we pulled up to the small park, there was no one there although the park was surrounded by homes.

We knew our music would be too loud. So I pulled my key leaders together and we decided to relocate to a park we were planning on going to next. We all got back into our cars and moved to Teague Park.

As soon as we pulled into the parking lot, I knew this was the place. I saw many homeless people hanging around the park's pavilions and wooded areas. We set up our equipment, clothes and grill for hot food. Our church's youth group came out to dance before the Lord and help us pass out tracts.

"This is going to be a great day," I thought to myself.

We had an average of at least a hundred people around our ministry area at any given time throughout the day. We were seeing a lot of ministry going forth and I was so excited.

God taught me another valuable lesson after deciding to enter into the ministry again.

Have you ever noticed that when you get a splinter in your finger, you will stop at nothing to find it and pull it out? Everything else is put on hold. Life will not go on until this hurt is dealt with. Why? The rest of your body is completely healthy. Ninety-nine percent of who you are is doing just fine. But it's that tiny little splinter that is causing pain and driving you crazy.

If you truly think about it, it has more to do with perspective and focus than it does with the pain. The more you focus on a problem, the larger that problem becomes to you. Your perspective will change. What at first is just a small speck of wood in your finger, but due to your focus on it, you changed your perspective to death! Initially your thoughts are, "Ouch! I need to pull that out."

Then you remain focused on it and your thoughts turn toward, "This is going to turn into an infection." Your perspective is now growing by the minute, "If I don't get this splinter out it will get infected and ultimately they will have to cut off my finger." Then the extreme sets in, "If that infection grows throughout my body I could die from this splinter."

At this moment, panic and anxiety are overwhelming you. Why? It all started with not staying focused on the task at hand but, instead, you've allowed yourself to make a mountain out of a mole's hill.

That splinter can represent any part of your life that is causing you pain. Although you may be blessed beyond measure in every other aspect of your life, there is one problem: you must remain focused. I truly believe this is why Paul teaches us in Philippians 4 that we are to remain focused on those things that are of a good report. Paul understood that through our focus on our problems, we can change our perspectives and make our problems larger than life.

Have you ever heard of the concept of mind over matter? I remember while playing football as a youth, there would be times when I would get hurt. Spraining an ankle, twisting a knee and even breaking a finger or two is not uncommon while playing a sport like football.

But what I remember the most were the few times when I would be lying on the field, agonizing in pain. I'm expecting my caring and compassionate coach to come running out on the field to me, rest my head in his lap and tell me ever so sweetly, "Everything is going to be alright."

Instead, I would wake up from my dream world to him hollering from the sideline, "Get up boy! You're alright! Play through the pain!" My coach also understood that although my pain was real, if I would get my mind back into the game, the pain would no longer be my focus.

Please understand, I know there are times when life needs to be put on hold for a time of healing. I just shared with you that I went through a time of sitting out the game and healing. I felt I was laying on the field with a broken arm and if I tried playing any longer, I would be hurting myself and my team even worse in the long run.

There are some trials in life that require us to sit some time out while we recover. But I also believe that we have to be very careful not to blow our pain out of proportion to where we are sitting on the sideline with a scrape on our toe while our coach, our team, our family and our church needs us playing. I have seen this too many times.

I know a man who has awesome talents and gifts, but chooses not to get involved in any type of ministry because 20 years ago a deacon told him to cut his hair. And if you ask him to join you in any ministry opportunity, he will tell you that he is through with church because they hurt him.

Give me a break! Get up and get in the game. Even if you have to play through a little pain, let your focus remain on the prize ahead. Don't let a splinter keep you sidelined.

Making Disciples

One of the frustrating things I had seen over the many years of doing these outreaches is that we always saw the same people over and over again. I remember pulling up to the parks and seeing them and thinking, "Didn't they give their heart to the Lord last time? Why are they still here with that bottle in their hands?"

We always tried to get our new converts plugged into local churches around the parks where we were ministering. But that strategy never seemed to work. Either the church would not follow up with the new convert or the new convert would never shadow the doorway of the church. Either way, I was increasingly growing frustrated with the lack of connection, change and discipleship in these people's lives. These feelings led me to do something I never dreamed I would do.

At Teague Park, we met a man named James. He was in his early fifties. He rode up on a pink bicycle with a beer in his hand. He was standoffish and just observed all the activity in the park. Besides, this was his home. He had a tent in the woods there and we were literally in his back yard. I noticed him, but just kept on with what I was doing. The next time I looked up, he is over in the middle of our area so I approached him.

"What's your name?" I asked.

"James. What's going on around here?" he responded.

I then explained that we were there to show him how much we cared about him. After a short conversation he knelt with me and my friend Phillip Briggs. James prayed the sinner's prayer. When we stood back up I asked him, "James, are you interested in coming out of this lifestyle? If you are, you can come home with me tonight."

I had to stop and recalculate what I had just said because it came out without me even thinking about it. I had not even spoken to my wife about it. I had made no preparation for where he would sleep, how much food he would eat, or what I was supposed to do with him once I got him there. All I knew was I didn't want to see history repeat itself. I just knew that the next time we would come to that park, there he would be: pink bicycle, beer in his hand and still living in a tent. He agreed to leave with me that night and seemed excited about the opportunity to change his life.

As the evening came we began to close the outreach down. I began looking around for James while tearing down our equipment. He was nowhere to be found. At first I thought we should wait for him because I just knew he wanted to come home with us but, as time passed, the reality of the situation set in.

Apparently fear, shame and other negative emotions had flooded his mind. I'm sure he thought that we were lying and betraying him as many others had. Or, he thought that we were looking to exploit him through free labor. These are real issues homeless people face. They get told many things by people who mean well but never follow through. I was disappointed but not discouraged. I had not forgotten what the Lord told me. I knew I would be going fishing again.

Beer and Tacos

A local church, Longview Christian Fellowship, invited my ministry team to minister in song during one of their men's meetings. We gladly accepted the invitation and set a date for July 24th and 25th which was about two weeks after our Party in the Park.

The first evening went great. We led the men in singing and gave a report of the great things God was allowing us to do. I also invited a good friend, Jennie Riddle, to join us. She has written many popular songs you hear on the radio and TV. After the service, we all decided to go across the street to have some tacos at Taco Casa, my favorite restaurant. Taco Casa and Don's Beer Barn share the same building; both are on opposite sides from each other. However, some will walk through the restaurant to get to Don's beer barn because of easier access.

While I'm making a mess of myself with taco sauce all

over my cheeks, lips and lap, in walks a man that Phillip recognizes. He is headed to Don's Beer Barn.

Phillip says, "Hey guys, I think that was James from the park."

I turn around, wiped my face and waited for him to walk back through.

Phillip says, "There he is!"

So I turned and called out to him as he was walking back through about to leave with a tall beer can in his hand.

"James!" I hollered.

"Hey! What's up guys?" James responded.

"Do you remember us from the park?" I asked. "I'm the one that tried to get you to come home with me."

"Sure I remember. I was just scared and didn't know what to expect so I decided to leave." James said.

After a little more small talk, I began another attempt to convince him to come with us. I told him about a local detox facility I could get him into for the night and that I would be there the next morning to pick him up. He wrestled with the idea for a while, but this time I was not going to take "no" for an answer. I finally convinced him to let us help him. He then gave me his beer. He had drunk very little of it.

I handed it Misty and said, "Here get rid of this, he doesn't need it anymore."

Misty replied, "What am I supposed to do with it?"

I said, "Throw it in the trash."

That was too much for James to handle at that moment. He ran over to the trash can, stuck his head in it, right in the middle of this restaurant, and began franticly digging for his beer. This time he was a little perturbed with me.

"I agreed to come with you guys, but I have to bring this beer with me to finish it. But this will be the last one I'll drink," James stated with a stern look on his face.

At this point, I didn't care. I just wanted to get him help. I asked him if he had anything he needed to get to take with him. He said he did and it was under a bridge behind the restaurant, which is where he was living at the time.

I was excited! Finally the cycle was going to be broken. Finally we were going to see change in someone's life, rather than a one-time experience.

Salt and "Jimmy" Pepper

"We are the light of the world. We are the salt of the earth. Everywhere we go, we should add the flavor of God to people's life. We should bring light into their darkness."

Those were my thoughts while walking through trash and mud and dodging tree limbs, headed toward the bridge. It was dark outside and I could barely see James walking in front of me.

Phil and I had left the others behind to go with James to retrieve his belongings. As we approached the side of the bridge and about to head underneath, a man and a woman came running out. He was dirty, only wearing jeans and was very muscular built. She was a very short, blond-haired woman and looked liked she had some mileage on her.

"Identify yourself!" he screamed while they were charging for us.

Fear gripped my whole being and they were coming at us fast and furious.

I started thinking, "They are coming up here to fight. I don't know how to fight! The last fight I was in was in the third grade with a first grader, and I did not win that one! This is going to hurt!"

I then began looking around for my escape when the thought hit me, "I only have to outrun Phil. They will settle for him." I knew I was faster than Phil.

They raced toward us and I was bracing for impact. Then they stopped right in front of us, nose to nose. I could smell bad breath and alcohol all over them. I was stiff as a board and sweating with fear.

At that moment James hollers, "Jimmy Pepper, they are with me. Leave them alone."

Still staring at me, he took a couple of steps back. I lifted my hand to shake his and began to introduce myself. "Hi! I'm Tim, this is Phil."

"Are ya'll the cops?" he asked.

"No," I said. "We are here to help James. Are you interested in getting help?"

I then noticed that behind Jimmy Pepper a fight had broke out between James and this little woman over the beer James was carrying.

"Give me that!" she grunted while trying to pull it away from James.

"Stop it!" Jimmy said as he turned toward them.

I looked at Phil and told him that we should just wait there instead of going any further. James, Jimmy and the little woman marched back under the bridge. Phil and I just stood there, relieved that we were still alive. A few minutes later, out popped James with a bag.

"Ya'll ready?" he asked.

"Let's go guys," I said.

As we were walking back up the hill, I couldn't help

but think about the living conditions where they were staying. What drives one so low that they believe a bridge is the best life has to offer them for a home? When does someone conclude in their heart that this is acceptable? My emotions were really moved at the sights and smells of that whole experience. I was more motivated than ever to reach as many people as I could to bring them hope. And although Jimmy Pepper was a rugged man, I knew he was still a man created by God, in the image of Christ. And that God loved him dearly.

We found out that Jimmy later went to prison for assaulting the woman who was with him. An investigator told me that Jimmy had beat her up pretty bad and that she had had enough and finally pressed charges against him.

Five-Mile Walk

We took James to a house that we heard helped men struggling with addictions. None of us knew much about it and had never been there before, but had only driven by it. We got him checked in and reassured him that we would be back the next morning to pick him up. We told him it would be after we completed the service we were involved with.

I woke up the next morning and began getting ready for the men's meeting. The whole time I had James on my mind and I was excited to go visit him.

I told Misty, "We need to pick him up for lunch and take him shopping for some new clothes. Let's see if he has ever had Starbucks."

We had caught our first disciple and I was ready to see a true transformation in his life.

The pastor began the service with opening remarks and prayer. I was standing behind the keyboard playing softly. After the prayer had concluded, my team and I began leading the men in congregational singing. Between playing the keyboard and leading the songs, I normally only glance at the audience so I can stay focused on hitting the right notes. There are still times when my fingers forget where they are supposed to land and I play a new "jazz note" that has never been written before (and probably shouldn't be).

About my third time to look up, I noticed someone walking in from the back. The platform lights were bright and the auditorium lights were dimmed so I couldn't make out the face right away. I kept my eyes on him because he looked familiar and it was obvious that he was headed toward the front.

As he got closer I noticed that it was James. Puzzled, I started wondering how he got there. But then, I started wondering if he was ever going to stop walking because he had made his way past the front row of chairs and was still coming toward the platform.

James walked all the way to the front edge of the platform and started shouting, "Where were y'all?" I looked around at my team and motioned for them to keep leading the song.

"I'm here! I made it! But where were y'all?" He asked.

I then walked around the keyboard and asked him, "James, what are you doing? How did you get here? You need to take a seat."

"I did it! I walked all the way here. It's about five miles, but I did it." he stated.

Seeing the determination in his eyes, my heart broke with compassion for him. I stopped the song and told the congregation the story of James and how we met. It was a God moment.

Men began to come out from their seats to meet James. Some prayed with him, others expressed love and grace. I was deeply moved by their response. I was even more touched that James would walk over five miles just to be with us in the service.

James continued to stay at the recovery house in the evenings and during the days he would hang around me or Phil. It was great getting to know him. I could tell at times that he would get uncomfortable with all the questions I was asking. I was not trying to pry, just trying to learn all I could about my new friend. But I later learned that when you have lived a hard lifestyle, as he had, there are some conversations that are too hurtful to talk about.

Chapter Five
Purpose

I believe the Word of God makes it clear that trouble-some times in our life are a part of God's plan. And we know God does nothing without purpose. Therefore, when we are facing troublesome seasons in our life, we can rest assured that there is purpose in our suffering. What I have found is that it not only makes the pain bearable to have this promise, but it changes your question from, "Why, God?" to "What, God?"

In addition to this, if you are better able to identify what the purpose is and what God is trying to accomplish, then you can, as the Bible says, "...count it all joy when you fall into divers temptations." You can rest in the promise that God is in control of your problems. He is a hands-on God who will be involved in your life as much as you will entrust it to Him. God will help you identify the purpose for the pain if you ask Him.

The Bible says that it is the Lord's good pleasure to speak with His children and to "reveal the mystery of His will."[46] He would not allow you to go through a trial without desiring for you to know His will and the purpose for the trial. It is not "tempting God"[47] to ask Him what's going on in your life. Tempting God would

---

[46] Ephesians 1:9
[47] Matthew 4:7

be running out in the middle of a busy highway during rush hour traffic and asking God to save you. But asking your Father to reveal to you the purpose in your pain is opening the heavenly channels in order to learn what it is He is trying to teach you.

If you are a parent, hope to be one, or able to use logic, then consider this: Would you ever walk into a child's room, discipline that child, and walk back out without saying one word during the whole ordeal? No, you would explain to the child why you feel it is necessary to address the issues in the child's life.

If I might borrow from Christ's words, "how much more does your heavenly Father..." who loves you even more than you can comprehend, wants to explain to you what it is that He has allowed. By learning, you can grow from it. God will only remain silent if He is never asked.

The pain I experienced at the church in Virginia was working for my good to make me a greater servant for Him. That pain crushed my will and brought me to a place of surrendering to His. The pain I experienced when my brother went to prison was working for my good. It brought great compassion into my heart for prisoners. Before my brother went in, I had the wrong attitude toward prisoners. I thought the state or federal government should lock them up and throw away the keys. There was no grace or mercy in my heart. The pain I felt while losing my marriage was working for my good. I now have a strong desire to help those that come from a broken home.

I can go on and on relating story after story, pain after pain to purpose, but the bottom line is that the pain was a part of the process of answering my prayer of "Lord, use me." God does not waste one moment of sorrow. It is all working together for our good according to Romans 8:28.

So ask Him. Ask God to help you identify the reason for your pain. God promises that He will answer you every time. He won't answer you according to your timing. But, in His time, you will know the answer and the purpose behind every heartache.

I believe there are many reasons for our pain. God caters according to our needs. Although there are many types of trouble that we face, I know all can be attributed and directly related to the calling on our life. In chapter one, we wrote about how sin in our life causes us pain. Let's consider some other purposes for our pain.

It's All Good
(Testing for a Greater Servant)

When you attend any form of educational classes, there are always exams that the teacher will give throughout the semester and school year. You normally have weekly tests, mid-term exams and the final exam. Tests and exams are meant to serve three purposes. First, the exams are given so the teacher and student can find out exactly which areas need improvement. Second, tests are also given to allow the students to apply what they have learned. And, third, tests are given to keep the students in check and alert.

As the student, you are aware that tests are just a part of your education, so you must pay close attention to your teacher. You cannot fall asleep during class and expect to pass the tests. You cannot daydream and take the class lightly because it will be only a matter of time before a test will come due.

Have you ever taken a closer look how God uses the word, "Test" throughout His Word? Obviously God has no need to give us a test for Him to know where we are because God is "all knowing."[48] There is nothing we do or even consider doing that escapes Him. But God will allow us to face tests for our own good.

The first chapter of James tells us to "...count it all joy when we fall into divers temptations." The word "temptations" actually means "tests." So why should I count it all joy? What's so fun about taking a test? Tests are hard. Tests require me to think about what I have learned. Tests challenge me.

Exactly! God does not want His servants to be stagnant and unwilling to grow. He does not want His servants to remain baby Christians, always drinking milk and never growing up to eat the meat of God's Word. "For though by this time you ought to be teachers, you need someone to teach you again the first principles of the oracles of God; and you have come to need milk and not solid food. For everyone who partakes only of milk is unskilled in the Word of Righteousness, for he is a babe. But solid food belongs to those who are full age, that is, those who by reason of use have their senses exercised to discern both good and evil."[49]

We should consider it an honor that the God of Heaven, creator of this universe and every creature within it, would be interested in someone like us. It should put a smile on our face when we realize that God has allowed a testing in our lives. He loves us enough to keep testing us in areas where we are weak in order to make us

---

[48] John 16:30
[49] Hebrews 5:12-14

stronger. In areas where our thinking is wrong (character flaws), He allows us to go through tests to correct our way of thinking. We should stand in amazement knowing that our God cares enough about us that He is helping us learn and grow throughout our lives. We should truly count it all joy.

I think it is interesting that God chose the word "fall" in James 1:2 to describe how we enter into a test or trial. It causes me to think of running on my road to destiny and going in the direction God has laid out for me. I'm trying to do everything right before the Lord. I have His map before me. I'm using His light for my path. But then all of a sudden – bam! I have fallen into a deep hole. I'm hurt and I feel all alone. Where is God? I don't feel Him near me anymore. What just happened to me?

The interesting thing about this analogy is that I was trying to do everything right. I was trying to be sensitive and hear His voice. I did not see anything I was doing wrong or that was a blatant sin. Why did God allow this hole to be in my path when I was headed in the direction He wanted me to go? Especially considering the fact I have been giving Him my time in prayer and service and have been faithful in giving of my tithes and offerings. I cannot understand why I should be going through this.

No, normally you cannot see it, but God can. God knows every part of you and knows where you need improvement. God "knows the hearts of men."[50] He is your creator. You are not here by chance or because your father took interest in your mother and they decided to have an intimate exchange.

---

[50] Acts 1:24

You were a gift of God to your parents. You were uniquely created and crafted by God. He is the one who gave you your own original DNA. He is the one who gave you your own unique fingerprints. "But the very hairs of your head are all numbered."[51] He is the one who keeps your heart beating. He is the one allowing you to face this trial you are going through. He is the one who has brought this book into your path so you would pick it up, read it, and understand that this trial is in your best interest.

You can find comfort in knowing that God has brought this about for your own good. And He will not allow you to fall so deep into the test that you are beyond His reach.

Read what David wrote in the fifth chapter of Psalms as he is reflecting back on his relationship with God: "O Lord, You have searched me and known me. You know my down sitting and mine uprising, you understand my thoughts afar off. You scrutinize my path and inspect all my ways, and are acquainted with all my ways. For there is not a word in my tongue, but You, O Lord, You know it altogether."[52]

Just like David, we should be able to relax and find rest in knowing that nothing takes God by surprise and He is the one in control. He is the one who inspects our ways and knows what to bring about in our lives to make the necessary corrections and improvements. These tests are increasing our anointing. These tests are taking us from "glory to glory."[53] These tests are "perfecting"[54] God's saints. "All things work together for the

---

[51] Matthew 10:30
[52] Psalms 139:1-4
[53] II Corinthians 3:18
[54] Psalms 138:8

good. . ."[55]

You Don't Know Like I Know
(Testimony for Witnessing)

Finding the glory of the Lord in our hardship always builds our faith but it also serves another purpose. It develops a testimony. How better to relate and minister to someone else's problem than to have walked through the same problem yourself. This is when God is molding you into a greater witness.

John 9 tells the story of a man who was blind from birth. As Jesus and His disciples passed by him, the disciples asked Jesus, "Master, who did sin? This man or his parents for him to be born blind?"

Jesus responded by saying, "Neither has this man sinned nor his parents; but that the works of God should be made manifested in him." Then Jesus spit on the ground and made clay. He anointed the man's eyes with the clay and told him to go wash. The man was able to see after washing his eyes.

What Jesus is saying here is that God allowed this man to be born blind. There was nothing he or his family did to cause this birth defect. God did not cause his blindness either, but God did allow it. God allowed it so that His healing power could be demonstrated through Jesus. The people around who were carefully watching could see the Son of God going about His Father's business and believed on Jesus as the Son of God.

Some of you reading this might find it hard to believe that God would allow someone to be born blind, or with other defects, just for the purpose of testimony. Well,

---

[55] Romans 8:28

consider this: God's ultimate goal is for everyone to
come to know Him and that all will be saved. So let me
ask you a question: If God himself came down, stood before you and asked if He could make you blind because
He knew your blindness and your testimony would
bring many to Him, would you allow it? Would you
take on this challenge? Or would you say, "No, I think
I'll pass. Give that challenge to someone else."

So what if everyone else decided to pass? Who would
God choose? You see, everyone is ministered to in different ways. Paul explained this when he said, "I become
all things to all people that I might win the more."[56]
What Paul is saying is that you are not going to reach
people by changing them first and then bringing them to
the Lord. No, you are going to win people by going to
them and touching them where they are. Jesus said to
"go out to the highways and hedges and compel them to
come in."[57] You must be willing to adapt and allow God
to use you and develop a testimony within you. This
way you can become a greater witnessing tool for advancing the Kingdom of Heaven.

Just consider your own life. Think about an addiction
you once had, a bad habit you had to break, or a poor
decision that ended up costing you dearly. What if your
next door neighbor came to your home and shared a
problem he or she was facing and it was a problem you
just experienced yourself. Is it possible to share with
them God's grace and deliverance from your firsthand
experience? Could you not tell this desperate person that
there is hope when you place your life in God's hands
and allow Him to guide you through this problem be-

---

[56] I Corinthians 9:19-23
[57] Luke 14:23

cause you just did? How many times have you been able to share your personal testimony with others? I'd venture to say, you have shared it many times.

Even if you cannot find any other reason for the adversity you are facing, you can know that God is developing a testimony within you. You will be able to say to yourself, "Wow, that was not easy to go through, but I thank God now that I have one more tool to use for His glory! Now I know He will be using me in a greater way."

Here is one last point concerning testimony. You can use it, not only as a witnessing tool to another, but as a witnessing tool to yourself. After the dust has settled and the smoke has cleared, after the storm clouds have dissipated and you catch a glimpse of sunlight, you will always remember the faithfulness of God in the midst of that trial. You will stand in God's sanctuary with a new outlook on His everlasting grace.

In the future, when undoubtedly you will face another trial, and your friends and family wonder how you are going to make it through this one without losing your mind, you can look them in the eye and say, "You don't know like I know. My God is faithful and He will not allow me to be tempted beyond what I can bear. And though I may walk through the valley of the shadow of death, I will fear no evil for God is with me." Amen!

Chapter Six
Fish Beget Fish

James was doing great. It seemed he was hungry to learn more about God. He was staying sober and attending church with us every Sunday. Everything seemed to be going well. Then one evening we dropped James off at the recovery house. He had been working all day doing yard work with us so he was anxious to get a shower. He gathered some clothes, saw that the bathroom door was unlocked and walked in. He caught another resident, named Jimmy Howard, with a needle in his arm, shooting up. James freaked out. He jumped on Jimmy fighting for the needle and trying to get Jimmy to stop. James took the needle and drugs away from Jimmy and called Phil.

"Phil, you have got to do something. This man needs help. I just found him shooting up."

"James, James, James!" Phil yelled, trying to interrupt James to make sense of what was being said.

James explained that Jimmy needed help from us. The recovery house was not helping him stay clean. And the more we went by the recovery house, the more often we noticed that there was no leadership there, ever! So James told Jimmy that the next morning he was going to go with him to meet us. We were going to pick them up and head to a Christian bikers rally called Spirit Rider where our outreach team was scheduled to play music.

We were running about 15 minutes late in picking them up. Jimmy seemed to be on edge with meeting new people, getting help and all the other unknown elements. So James was concerned that Jimmy was going to run off. James' fears were realized right before we showed up. Jimmy ran behind the house and hid in a wooded area. Another guy was behind there too who had crack. Jimmy shot up again.

James was devastated. We decided to drive around for a little while and see if we could find Jimmy. After a few minutes, we spotted him walking behind a Whataburger in the woods, a short distance from our house. James jumped out of my truck, ran over to Jimmy and somehow convinced him to come with us. We had an RV that we used for our outreaches so we let him go into the RV and shower and get cleaned up before the event. All throughout the day, Jimmy never spoke a word. He never cracked a smile. And he would never look us in the eye.

Not really knowing what to do next with these guys, we took James and Jimmy back to the recovery home. James assured us he would watch after Jimmy. But just in case, I called one of the leaders of the recovery home and shared what happened in hopes he would watch after the place more carefully. That didn't happen.

Jimmy started coming around little by little. He had stopped relapsing and started hanging with us every day. He was going to church with us each week and actually started to smile occasionally.

During this time we also met a young black man named Lamont. Pretty. Soon, we had all three of them with us each day. Phil and I really didn't know what to do with them, but we just knew that as long as they were with us, they were not high on drugs and their needs were being met.

Every evening we would drop them off to stay the night at the recovery home and would pick them back up the next morning. Through James, we were able to reach out to two more men and help them become followers of Christ.

Fishing in the Perfect Storm

On August the 9th, we planned another Party in the Park outreach. It was another great day of ministry. This time, people learned about all the free food, clothes and music. The park looked packed. I picked up some tracts and my Bible and walked around talking to as many people as would listen.

A very rugged looking man named Mac was sitting under one of the pavilions. I walked up to him, sat down and started talking about the weather, music and great food. That led into me sharing Christ with him and after a lengthy discussion, Mac gave his heart to the Lord. Once again, without thinking about it, I asked him to let us help him. He agreed and came over to our ministry area where he stayed, ready to leave with us.

I also met four more people who wanted to make a lifestyle change: Ruby, Eric, Tina and Donald. At the close of the outreach, it dawned on me, "O.K. Tim. You now have five more people, in addition to the three you already have, looking to you for help. What are you going to do?"

I didn't have a plan. I didn't know what to do. I just had a compassion for helping them and trusted that God would somehow help me work it out.

Phil and I discussed our options and came up with a plan to at least get us through the evening. We decided we would take Mac's car to the church to drop it off since we knew that we would be at church the following morning. After gathering a plan for Mac's car, he then revealed that he had a dog in the car that needed a place to stay.

"Come on, Mac. We will provide shelter for people, but I don't see us being an animal shelter, too," I told him.

"If my dog doesn't go, then I don't go," Mac assured me.

As my mouthed opened and my finger lifted to respond to Mac's demand, Caryn, a friend of mine, stepped in and said she would take the dog home with her. I shook my head and walked away.

Our plan was then to get them a hotel room for the night and pick them up the next morning for church. After discussing our plan, I told Misty, "Right now, we are not living from day to day, but rather moment by moment."

Whatever Suits Your Fancy

Mac was very hesitant to let Caryn take his dog, Fancy Lady, home with her. Fancy was all Mac really had in life. We told him that Caryn is an animal lover and will take great care of the dog. After a while, we convinced him that everything would be fine.

"Besides Mac, what could possibly go wrong? She will take good care of Fancy for you," I said with confidence.

"She better, because Fancy is all I got," Mac said with that, "I'm watching you," look on his face. Mac then turned to Caryn and said, "Don't let anything happen to my dog."

When Mac got into the car to leave for the hotel, we all joked about how serious he was about Fancy. We couldn't think of one thing for Mac to worry about. Boy, were we wrong.

Fancy was riding in the lap of Caryn's daughter as she pulled out of the park and started driving down Highway 80. All of the sudden, Caryn's daughter hollers from the back of the van, "Mom, she jumped out!"

Caryn whips over to the side of the road to find that Fancy had jumped out of the window, onto the highway at a high rate of speed. Panic set in and they began frantically looking for Fancy. They spotted her limping down the road. Caryn just knew that Fancy must have been hit by a car.

They chased Fancy down the road a ways, but as they got closer, Fancy darted into a wooded area and they lost her. They ran back to the van and started driving around the area looking for Fancy. They just knew Mac would kill us all if he found out Fancy had got hit by a car, was lost and maybe even dead.

After searching for what seemed like eternity, Caryn found Fancy at the Globe hotel. Mac had stayed there from time to time so Fancy knew to return to that place in hopes of finding her master.

I was standing in line at the hotel with Mac and the others behind me, ready to check them in. My phone rings and I see that it's Caryn. I could tell by her voice that something was wrong.

"You are not going to believe what happened to

Mac's dog," she said.

My heart sank into my shoes. I looked back at Mac, smiled and told them in a whispering voice, "I'll be right back. This is an important call."

"Tim, the dog jumped out of the window of my van. I think she got hit by a car. She is whining and has a bad limp," Caryn begins to explain. "What do you want me to do?"

"I have no idea! Just try to keep the poor thing alive until I can muster up the courage to tell Mac," I told her.

I walked back to the counter slowly and told the clerk I need some rooms for the evening. I didn't dare look back at Mac in fear that he would see that something was wrong. Only prayer and fasting was going to give me the strength I needed to face Mac on this one.

I got them checked in and ran to my truck to call Caryn back. She finally made it home, but told me that the dog was shaking, would not eat and still had a bad limp. My life started flashing before my eyes.

I started thinking that I need to get my house in order before I tell Mac because I might not be going back home. We decided to see how Fancy did throughout the night. We thought we could tell him at church the next morning. We were hoping that mercy would flood his soul during the service and we could catch him at just the right time.

The next morning we drove to the hotel to pick up the five of them. As I'm pulling up, Donald meets me at the door of his room. He had already gone that morning to get a beer and was drinking it. I asked him if he was ready to go to church with us.

"Yes I am. I'm tired of living this way," Donald said.

I told him that the beer couldn't come with us to

church.

"That's ok. I'm through with this stuff anyway," he said.

Donald then pours it out in front of me.

"Where are the rest of them?" I asked.

"Ruby and Eric left during the night. Mac is sitting out by the pool," Donald said.

I walked out to the pool and there was Mac, sitting in a chair smoking.

"Good morning Mac," I cheerfully said.

"I'm not ready for this, Tim. I can't change. I've tried. I've been living this way all of my life. I don't think there is any hope for me," Mac said while staring at the pool.

I knelt down beside him and said, "Mac, there's hope for everyone. No, you can't change on your own, but if you surrender your life to Christ, He will do it for you."

He stood up, put out his cigarette and said, "Well, let's go."

On the way, Tina began acting very weird with her body language and every word she said was slurred. Donald and Tina then started arguing and I heard her say loudly, "Let me out of this truck!" I pulled over to the side of the road and she got out. Donald was upset that she was leaving but he stayed, determined to get help.

Before church began, Phil and Mac were standing at the front where their seats were. Caryn walked up, greeted everyone and as she approached Mac he asked, "How is my baby girl doing?"

Caryn stuttered around a little and finally just told him what had happened. She finished by saying, "I think Fancy was hit by a car because she is walking with a bad limp."

Mac smiled and said, "She has had a bad hip for years. She didn't get by a car!"

Phil and Caryn were both relieved and speechless. When Phil told me what Mac said, I pulled out the sheet of paper in my pocket where I was writing down my will, and tore it up.

"Thank the living, Lord Jesus!" I exclaimed.

Proud Moment of Faith

Service was awesome and all of the people we brought accepted the pastor's invitation to come down for prayer. It seemed everyone was full of joy and excited about what God had done in their life. I had been serving full-time in the ministry for over 10 years at this time. I had been a believer for over 25 years. Yet I cannot remember being more proud of my faith in Christ than this day. My spiritual chest was out and my head was held high. Not because of what I had done. No! I was proud of what God had done in me. I knew that God had changed my life, so that I could help bring change to another's life.

After church, we decided to take the men to the recovery home along with James, Lamont and Jimmy. But Donald refused to go there. He wanted to be dropped off on the streets again. Mac wanted to be taken to a local transitional housing facility. I was okay with their decisions this time. Disappointment did not get the better of me. I knew that the seeds of God's Word had been planted in their hearts and I would see them again, soon.

Chapter Seven
Birthing Pains

The next few weeks, Phil and I stayed in the same routine. We would pick up James, Jimmy and Lamont. We would have a Bible Study with them sometime throughout the day and take care of their needs. We were seeing real change. Oppression had left. Chains were breaking off. And these men were being released and freed from the bondages that had enslaved them for years.

It's 2 a.m. I get a call from a local bar. "Is this Tim?" a man asked on the other end.

Half awake I replied, "Yeah, this is Tim. Who is this?"

"I have a young man in my bar that is causing all kinds of trouble. He is drunk and I'm about to call the police. But he said he knew you, and that you would come pick him up. It's either you come get him, or he is going to jail," the bartender said.

I asked him where the bar was located and told him that I would be on my way.

Normally, I would think that sitting it out in jail might be a good wake-up call for someone. But this was different. This was Donald who had over 50 public intoxications on his record already and was only 21 years old. Donald had had one of the hardest lives of anyone on the streets. At the age of 13, he began being molested by his father. He did not tell anyone, not even his mom that this was happening.

However, one day at his school, the faculty noticed some things wrong with him. He was sent to the nurse's office. His mother was called by the school and did not believe the evidence or Donald's story that his father was raping him. Instead, she turned all her anger toward him.

His father was later convicted and sent to prison, where he still is to this day. His mother remarried but still carried resentment toward Donald. She thought he was the cause of her losing her first husband. After a couple more years, his mom kicked him out of the house.

Here Donald was, in his early teenage years, homeless, nowhere to go and no one to turn to. He began drinking and doing drugs. He found a place to live in a tent in the woods. He made money by any means possible for food and to feed the addiction to drugs and alcohol.

You Can't Choose Who You Will Love

Here I was, a local pastor, 2 a.m. in the morning, about to walk into a bar. I was praying that none of my church members would see me. But then I reasoned, if someone did, they would ask me the question, "Well… what are you doing down here, PASTOR?"

I would then respond with the same question. Then maybe we could settle on, "If you won't say anything, neither will I." But even that was shady at best, so my nerves began to kick in full throttle.

I have never been to a club in all my life. I didn't

know what to expect. And to make it worse, as I'm approaching the door to this club I noticed a sign. It read, "If you are offended by gay or homosexual activity, do not enter." I looked above the door and there was a big rainbow. I immediately turned around and got back into my truck to leave. I didn't mind walking into a bar to get Donald, but this was asking too much of me. I can't go that far.

I started my truck and was headed to the edge of the parking lot when I heard that soft voice of the Lord say to me, "You can't choose who you love." My head fell back onto the seat. I knew what I had to do. I parked the truck again and walked on through the front door of the club.

I took one step inside and stopped to look around. It was smoky and loud music was blaring. Straight ahead of me was the bar. I looked to the left and it was a lounge area where people were doing things not suitable to mention for this book. I then looked to my right and it was a game area with a couple of pool tables, pinball machines, etc. As I looked closer, I saw Donald standing by one of the pinball machines talking to a man with a beer in his hand.

I walked over to him and said, "Donald, you need to come with me." I got us out of there as fast as I could.

My plan was to take him to a local detuning facility called Oak Haven. We arrived and I noticed that Donald was already passed out in the driver's seat. I woke him up and he stumbled to the door with me.

The whole way to the door he was telling me, "I'm not staying here. I'm not staying here."

At this point, I'm fairly upset. Here I am trying to help this guy at 2 a.m., away from my family, saving him from going to jail, and he is telling me what he is going to do?

I stopped, stuck out my arm to stop him, "Donald, look at me. You are going to stay where ever I want you to stay. You are not in any condition to make a decision right now, anyway."

He looked at me and smirked, "I said...I isn't going in there."

I turned toward the door and started walking inside. I thought that if they saw him in this condition they would take him in whether he wanted to or not. As I reach the front counter, a man asked if he could help me.

"Yes sir, I have a man outside that needs help. He is totally wasted," I said.

The man then informed me that there were no beds available. They were totally full.

I decided that he would just have to stay at the recovery house that night.

"Get in Donald," I told him as I was exiting the building.

"See, I told you I wasn't staying here tonight," Donald smarted off.

I was ready to take him to jail myself at that point. We drove over to the recovery house and I knocked on the front door. No answer. I tried calling the house. No answer. I tried calling the leader's cell phone. No answer. I repeated this process many times trying to get someone to the door, still nothing. I went back to my truck and saw that Donald was passed out again. I put the truck into drive and started pulling away. I didn't even know where I was driving to. I turned into a grocery store parking lot, my head fell onto the steering wheel and I started crying uncontrollably.

I prayed, "God, what am I supposed to do now? Where am I supposed to take him? I can't put him out on the streets. Someone will surely take advantage of him in this condition. Jail is not the answer. The local hospital won't take him since he is refusing."

I was totally lost and desperate for God to help me with this situation. My mind went back to the scripture in Isaiah 58:7 "...bring to your house the poor who are cast out." Then my thoughts turned toward Matthew 25:43, "When I was a stranger, you took me in."

I looked over at Donald and heard a whispering voice say, "What would you do if that was me sitting there?" My eyes flooded once again. "What you do to the least of these, you are doing unto me."

I prayed, "But God, what about my family? What about my children? I don't know this man. I don't know what he is capable of doing? I'm scared, God!"

God replied, "Would I ask you to do something that would hurt you or your family? I'm your refuge. I'm your strong tower. I'm your protector."

My home has always been my safe haven. It was not too often that I had friends come over. I was around people who needed my attention so much through the day that home was my escape. I always wanted to keep my home to my family and to myself. But this time God was showing me that my home needs to be a safe haven for Donald tonight, too.

So I brought Donald to my house. I helped him get out of my truck and onto a chair. I got a blanket and pillow made out the couch for him to sleep on. I helped him get onto the couch where he passed out again. I sat across from him and prayed that God would protect us that night.

I then walked into my kids' room and locked their door, locked our hallway door and locked my bedroom door behind me. I didn't get any sleep that night. Every little sound I heard woke me up and I would get up to check on it.

The next morning Donald remembered nothing about the events from the night before. I fixed breakfast for him and after laying down some ground rules, Donald started living with us.

Five Men, Five Mats

After a while, Mac began to stay at the recovery house with our other guys and hanging out with us during the day. One night, a few hours after dropping the guys off, we got a phone call from Mac saying that James was acting crazy and had climbed a tree. Phil was with me when we got the call. We took Donald out there with us to see what was going on. We got there and sure enough, there was James high up in a tree.

Phil hollered at James to come down.

James said, "No! Mac relapsed and is threatening me."

During all the commotion with Mac and James, Donald and Jimmy snuck off to a gas station around the corner from the house to get some weed.

We finally talked James into coming down out of the tree. About that time, we noticed that Donald and Jimmy were gone.

James said, "I know where they went. I'll go get them."

James found them, but then decided to have a few beers with them there. Later we found out that James was the one that had been drinking all along. That night, not only did all of our guys relapse, but everyone in the recovery house had relapsed as well.

We were very frustrated that this had happened. We should have seen it coming because this recovery house was poorly managed and had no accountability for the men. Plus, this house was in the heart of all the drug activity. Directly across the street was a road known by all drug dealers and users as "Crack Ally." We realized that we could not leave the men we were trying to help there any longer. There was too much temptation and opportunity.

That night, I brought Donald, Mac, Jimmy and James home with me to stay. We would put out mats at night for them to sleep. During the day they would go with me or Phil and in the evenings we would have a Bible study over dinner. We also developed some extra-curricular activities for them to be involved in – concerts, putt-putt golf, fishing, etc. Lamont remained at the recovery house for a few more days before moving in with us as well.

Jumping Off a Cliff

There are several hundred homeless people in Longview and Gregg County on any given day. For a small town, compared to Dallas, Houston and Austin, we are heavily populated with those needing shelter. Even greater needs than sheltering are programs for those wanting help with their addictions.

A high percentage of families across America are affected one way or another by an addiction. Maybe you are struggling with an addiction, or a family member, or a friend, or a co-worker, or a neighbor. If you are not directly affected, more than likely you know someone who is. Since starting to help men with addictions, my eyes were opened to the great need in our communities for recovery programs.

We began to get calls from mothers, fathers, brothers, and lawyers with clients addicted to drugs. We felt overwhelmed at times. We wanted to do more, but didn't know what to do or where to turn. We just continued to disciple the men we had and prayed for direction from God.

Out of the blue, I received an email from a member of my church wanting me to let anyone know in the church that she had a house for sale. Her friend named Deena had passed away after battling cancer. She stated that Deena and her friend Kathy lived there, but with Deena passing, Kathy could no longer afford it.

I replied back with a few questions. I believe she thought I was gathering more information to post at the church, but actually I was inquiring for my men to have a place to live. And maybe bring more men in.

I set up a meeting with Kathy at the house on Fox Lane. We discussed all our options, but settled on a lease-purchase agreement. Misty and I decided to stretch our resources further. We knew it would be a giant leap of faith for us financially.

In my prayer time, I told God that it felt like He was asking me to jump off a cliff. He responded with, "Go ahead, jump!" And I knew in my heart God would catch me every time if He is the one telling me to take this step of faith. We were so excited that I really was not that concerned. I just knew within me that God would provide.

This was our first discipleship home. We called the home Deena's House of Disciples, in her honor. Misty and I knew that God had called us to this special ministry. Phil and his wife Jennifer moved into the house on Fox Lane on Labor Day weekend and all five of our men moved in with them.

Earth, Wind and "Fired"

An old childhood friend of mine kept coming to mind while this ministry was evolving. His name was Trey and we were really close growing up. After I moved off to college, I stayed in touch with him and learned that he had his struggles with drugs. He had also spent time in prison for various crimes.

It had been a few years since I spoke to him, but I decided to try to reach him. Who knows, maybe he is doing great and could come up to Longview to help us. Plus, we could use all the help we could possibly get. The last I had heard, he was living in the Austin area, so I looked him up on the internet and found his dad's number. I called and left a message on his voice mail letting him know that I would like to get in touch with Trey.

A couple of days passed and Trey calls me back. It was so good to hear from him. I remember that I smiled throughout the whole conversation. After catching up on some old times, I share with him what God has been doing with our new discipleship program. Trey then tells me that he is running a program in Austin.

Without any hesitation I asked, "How 'bout you coming up here and helping me get this one up and running. I don't know what I'm doing here."

Within a couple of weeks, Trey came up to visit. He had not changed a bit. Still a lot of fun to be around and looked just like he had growing up. I showed him our new home and walked him through what we were doing. He had a lot of input and I was impressed by everything he said.

After a few days, I was convinced that he could bring insight and structure to us so I asked him to consider becoming a part of our team. He returned to Austin, packed up and came right back to Longview.

Trey came in with guns blazing. The first item on his agenda was to sit down with the men and lay down the law. We had always been fairly easy with the guys. We didn't have many rules. Basically they were like family and we treated them as such, but trusting Trey knew what he was doing, I let him take the reigns.

It was a shock for the guys to have this six-foot, four-inch man standing over them drilling them over what all they can and cannot do. I was convinced we needed guidelines and rules for the residents, but I was not convinced that it needed to be presented to them this way. However, Trey told me that he ran a program in Austin before coming up, so I just kept reminding myself of that.

With Trey now on board, it seemed we had sufficient leadership in place. I decided I would plan a getaway for my family a couple of months out. It had been a few years since we made time to break away from the everyday challenges. I also invited Phil and Jennifer to go with us. We thought it would be a good time to reflect and pray about where God is taking us next.

We selected a cruise out of Galveston, Texas. We were all pumped and looking forward to spending a week out on the water. My children had never been on a cruise before. Our plans were to leave out Saturday, drive the four hours there and spend the rest of the day on the beach. We would wake up the next morning and hop on the cruise ship which was scheduled to leave at 3 p.m., Sunday, September 13th.

On Thursday, September 9th, hurricane Ike made landfall near Galveston as a strong Category 2 hurricane, with a Category 5 equivalent storm surge. East Texas was in a direct line with it and Ike was approaching fast. We began getting ready for it by stocking up on food, candles, flash-lights, etc. On Saturday, the hurricane hit East Texas. Winds were swirling around very forcefully, trees were tumbling over and the electricity went out immediately.

It's in moments like these that you are reminded of how powerful God is. We had a generator to keep the refrigerator going and some lights on. We opened up our home to some neighbors who had lost their electricity.

Galveston was hit pretty hard, too, so Misty and Jennifer started calling and looking at our cruise line's website to check on the status of our vacation. They kept telling us that no decision had been made yet. After continually researching, they finally got the answer Saturday night, our cruise was cancelled.

Disappointed, but understanding the situation, we huddled together and made the decision to try to find something else to do, but not cancel our time away. We spent all day Sunday figuring out alternate plans for our vacation.

Have you ever tried to get four adults, a five-, an eight- and a nine-year-old to agree on anything? Needless to say, it took all day, but we finally settled on renting a house boat in Arkansas. Now the plan is to leave first thing Monday morning. However, another hurricane hit, just in a different form.

Late Sunday night, Mac tells Trey that he needs to do laundry and since the electricity is still out, he will need to leave the house for a local laundry mat. After a couple of hours, we start getting concerned. Another hour passes and we are now trying to figure out where he is. Two more hours pass and Mac shows back up drunk. Being late, Phil went on to bed to let Trey handle the situation with Mac. Plus, tomorrow was the big day for leaving for our vacation. Phil also assumed that the policy Trey put in place would be enforced, which is that a "relapse while in the program is grounds for immediate dismissal."

Phil woke up Monday morning and noticed that his truck was gone. Since Trey didn't have any transportation, it was not unusual for Trey to use his truck to run errands. Then Phil gets a call from Mac asking him to come get him that he needed help and that he had a story to tell us.

Phil replies, "Mac, do you know where my truck and Trey are?"

Slowly and with caution Mac replies, "That's actually what I want to talk to you about." Mac goes on to explain that instead of Trey asking him to leave the program, Trey jumps in Phil's truck with him to go to a strip club. They both stayed out all night getting drunk and at some point during the night, Trey left Mac at the club, and ran off with a prostitute to smoke crack. At this point, Phil really didn't know whether Mac was telling the truth or not.

I'm at home getting everything packed in the car and

ready to go on our family vacation. I had created a checklist and was marking them off one by one. I had all our bags loaded and was about to head back inside the house to start on a good breakfast when my phone rang. I noticed it was Phil and my first thoughts were that he wanted to know the exact time we were leaving.

But instead Phil said, "Tim, we got a problem. Mac has relapsed and he is saying that Trey has, too. My truck is gone and I'm not sure whether to believe Mac's story or not."

I told Phil, "I'm on my way."

I jumped in the car and headed across town to Fox Lane. I picked up Phil and we went to get Mac and maybe make some sense of all this. I try calling Trey's phone but it kept going straight to voice mail. We go back to Fox Lane and again ask Mac to tell us what happened.

During this time, Trey calls us from a local Caterpillar dealer asking us to come meet him. He says he has a story to tell about Mac. Trey goes on to explain how Mac needed a ride since being kicked out that night, and had led Trey to some far away place in the woods. He said that Mac jumped out, ran off and left him lost and out of gas. And that Mac had stolen his phone.

I knew that Trey was new to Longview, but nothing else he said made sense. Phil and I go to meet Trey and it was apparent at first glance of him that he was stoned. He was denying that he had done anything wrong, but we knew better. I was totally devastated.

Not knowing what to do from here, I tell Trey to get in the truck and we made the quiet trip back to Fox Lane. Here I am, my family is counting on me to go on vacation, yet my leader of the program has just relapsed.

Phil and Jennifer were planning on going, too, which would leave us without a leader at the house. As soon as we walked in the front door, I knelt down on the couch and started crying and praying to God for direction and help.

After a short time of praying, I heard someone hollering behind me. I turn around startled and I see Trey walking back and forth and he seems to be praying. Then I noticed that Mac and Phil had also knelt down to pray. I turn to pray again and Trey hollers again from the kitchen at the top of his lungs.

This time I could make sense of what he screamed, "God, why won't you heal me?"

I got up and walked over to him, gave him a hug and began to explain that God's healing only comes through us relying on Him, rather than God waving His magic wand and suddenly we no longer have any problems.

Later I took Trey to Isaiah 58:8 and spoke to him about focusing our lives upon other people and how that brings healing to us. In the end, we sat Trey and Mac down and the truth finally came out that Mac's story was indeed the truth. Trey admitted to relapsing, selling his phone for drugs and using Phil's truck for all the wrong reasons. I informed Trey that he was no longer on staff and that he could stay, but now only as a man in the program. My thoughts shifted toward helping him.

Love Thy Neighbor

They went to sleep after talking to me and Phil. I decided that I needed to stay behind and let everyone else go ahead and leave for vacation. There was no reason for anyone else to have to miss out on their vacation. Phil,

Jennifer and Misty and my children left later that morning for Arkansas. I felt overwhelmed because of all that had just taken place. I'm not sure how much rest I would have gotten anyway. I'm sure my mind would have played out the weekend's events.

I stayed with my guys on Fox Lane, only to go home to feed the animals and check the mail. Looking back, I now can see how God gave this opportunity to isolate me to focus on Him and this ministry.

I spent the whole week in prayer and thought. The rest I would have had on vacation, I actually found in Jesus that week. God showed me areas of improvement and gave me new vision. I soon realized that it was vital for me to be in town to handle another major issue that would come up during the week. Also, in chapter 4, I shared how God gave me a scripture for our outreach team found in Luke 5:4, "Launch out into the deep for a great catch." This week was the three-year anniversary of that Word from the Lord. And what is happening? We now have a great catch. Now God has to show us how to clean them.

Tuesday morning was a beautiful day. I got up feeling rested and ready to tackle the day with God's grace. So I poured a bowl of cereal, fixed a cup of coffee, with lots of cream and sugar, and sat out back on the porch to read. I went back into the house after a while and noticed I had a voice mail. It was from the City of Longview. The neighbor next door had complained to the city about our dogs barking.

However, that opened a huge can of worms because one of our guys decided to take it upon himself to tell the neighbor all about who is living beside her. I'm sure he had good intentions, but it had the opposite effect.

She calls the city back again and tells them that we have numerous people living there and that the conditions of our living arrangements were very poor.

Now the city calls and informs me that I'm facing fines and possible charges for violating occupancy codes. I told them I was very sorry and didn't know what the codes were, but I would make it right. Only four men could live at this location and I had one week to reduce our current 12 men to four.

The first thing I felt I needed to do was to make it right with our neighbor. So I walk next door and rang the doorbell. A middle-aged woman answered the door with her arms folded and she had a look on her face that would scare the strongest of men. I stuck out my hand to introduce myself, but she looked down at it, looked back up at my face and shut the door. Not sure why, maybe glutting for punishment, I rang the doorbell again.

She came back to the door and opened it just far enough to yell at me, "Go away!"

She then shut the door in my face again. Defeated, I walked back to the house like a dog with its tail between its legs, but I knew that this was not over yet. I was determined to reach her.

The next day, I got up and drove to buy the most beautiful flowers I could find. When I got back, I snuck over to her front porch and put the flowers on her steps. I noticed that later in the evening the flowers were gone. She had taken them in with her. All I could do was smile.

Thursday, I walk back over to her house and ring the doorbell. She opened the door and stood in the same posture as before. Her arms folded and a look that could kill, but without me saying a word, just standing there with a goofy grin on my face, she reluctantly invited me in the house.

I didn't speak one word for the next 10 to 15 minutes. She started by telling me that she doesn't want those "types" of people living next to her. She went on to explain that all these "types" of people do is steal, trash their home and act crazy. As she began to wrap up her speech about how bad of people we are, I finally asked her a question.

"Ma'am, what makes you feel this way about these men? Where is all of this coming from?" I asked. "It seems very personal to you."

She paused for a moment, turned away from me and sat back in her chair. While staring straight ahead, she said, "It's my son." She continued, "He is homeless, living on the streets addicted to meth. He has robbed me blind. He has stripped me of any dignity I had. Every good thing I have tried to do for him, he has taken advantage of it and used it to further indulge in his addiction."

We continued discussing her son at length. My heart broke for her and what she had gone through. I told her that I loved her and asked if we could pray. She agreed. We held hands and prayed for her son to be restored and healed, as well as her.

Everything was resolved with our neighbor from that time forward. I stopped by to visit with her occasionally to see how she was doing. During one of those visits, she gave me some information about her son so I could try to contact him for help. I tried multiple times to pursue his whereabouts, but never could find him.

I had read the scripture in the Bible that says, "Pray for those that despitefully use you and do good to them that hate you." But I had never really had to exercise it in a situation before. God gave me that opportunity and I'm grateful for it. I learned some valuable lessons that are now applied to my life. My faith in God's Word was strengthened. Also, we saw God working all things out for our good.

As a result of our neighbor's complaining to others in our neighborhood, a family across the street inquired about our ministry because they had a daughter that was homeless and addicted to drugs. I was allowed to share our ministry with them and their response was excitement. A few weeks passed and they felt led to donate a 1989 Lincoln Town Car to us.

Although we had reconciled the relationship with our neighbor next door, we still had the dilemma of finding another place to house our men. I continued to correspond with the city and they were willing to work with us. We still needed to move the men, but the city had lifted the urgency to relocate.

So by staying obedient to God in handling the situation with the lady next door, God honored our efforts in many ways. I finished out the week with the guys at Fox Lane until everyone returned back from vacation.

Chapter Eight
It's in the Process

There used to be a time when we had no cell phones, believe it or not. I'm old enough to remember when you actually had to leave a message and wait for someone to call you back. I remember driving down the road and needing to call someone, so I'd pull over and put 25 cents into a pay phone. Today, pay phones are almost nonexistent.

I remember a time when I had to balance my check book to know what was in my checking account. Now I send a text to my bank and immediately receive a text back with my balance. I remember when my car was a lot easier to fix if something broke down. Now I open the hood and all I see are wires, computers and a whole lot of confusion. I remember a time when everyone had to sit down at a restaurant if you wanted something to eat, rather than the "fast food" we have now.

All this is amazing to me because our society has invented these conveniences and technologies to make life easier and save us time. If you truly consider what has happened, it has caused the opposite effect. Although we live in an age where most everything is instant, society is busier than ever before. We have added much technology to the "reinvention of the wheel" to make life more convenient, yet society is more complex than ever before.

Don't get me wrong, I enjoy the latest gadgets that have come out. I'm not sure how to use them half the time, but once I figure out how to turn them on, they're a lot of fun to use. But I do remember when life was simple. I do remember when life was lived at a slower pace.

The world we live in today teaches us to not have patience. My generation does not have to wait for anything. We try our best to avoid the process of waiting and just go ahead and get. If we want the latest gadget and don't have the funds on hand, we fill out the application for credit and off we go paying up to 300 percent more than what it was retailed for. Why? The reason is society has given us every opportunity to escape waiting and saving up little by little for what we want or need.

Credit card companies are not making money on great business plans, they are making money on our impatience. They bank on knowing that we will do any and everything to get what we want – now. Just as some companies make money off of instilling fear into buying their product.

For example, "If you don't buy the latest fire alarm for your washer, it will blow up when you are not watching, then burn you and everyone on your block up." I have actually had a door-to-door salesman tell me that. Credit card companies market their product, instant money, knowing that this generation will not go through the process of saving our money and paying cash.

I have seen this in my own life and in the life of many men and women that have come to House of Disciples for help. When we tell them that our program is for 12 months, they turn around and walk thinking they don't need to be tied down for 12 months.

In Longview, there is a 30-day detoxifying facility. I have seen many people check into this facility, finish their 30 days and believe they are clean. I have never personally witnessed any remaining clean. Each one of them relapsed shortly after leaving. Why? They wanted instant results instead of going through the process of healing. They want healing on credit, believing they can pay it off over time. But there are some things in life that will put you in a cycle of insanity until you come to the end of yourself, and decide you are going to go through the process.

It's in the process of trials like financial difficulties, broken families and illnesses that we find and develop the character traits we need to become all that God has called us to be. The very thing we keep trying to avoid, due to lack of patience and trust in God, is the very thing God keeps sending us back to – process. The meaning of the word "process" is the act of taking something through an established and usually routine set of procedures to convert it from one form to another.

Eleanor Roosevelt once stated, "People grow through experience if they meet life honestly and courageously. This is how character is built." What she is saying is that it is in the process that we build character and faith. God desires to take us through His Kingdom procedures to convert us from glory to glory.

As a matter of fact, God even outlines the exact process He desires to take us through in II Peter 1:5-10, "But also for this very reason, giving all diligence, add to your faith virtue, to virtue knowledge, to knowledge self-control, to self-control perseverance, to perseverance godliness, to godliness brotherly kindness, and to brotherly kindness love. For if these things are yours and abound, *you will be* neither barren nor unfruitful in the knowledge of our Lord Jesus Christ."

What Do Apples and Oranges Have in Common?

God wants His children to be fruitful and multiply. When He sees us getting stagnate and not producing, He will allow us to go through the process of pruning.

Let's take a closer look at this. The first words we notice are "… but also for this very reason." He is saying that in addition to the promises made to us when we receive Christ as our Lord and Savior, we need to go through this process to become fruitful in our faith to Him.

The next phrase we read is "giving all diligence." The word "Diligence" in the Greek is *spoudē* which means "*w*ith haste, earnestness in accomplishing, promoting, or striving after anything." He is teaching that we should strive hard to add the character traits we find in the process to our lives. We should not try to skip the process, but with patience in the Lord, waiting on Him by faith, we go through the fire knowing that He is right there with us.

The next word we read is "add." We need to understand that in the process, these godly traits are being stacked upon each other, layer by layer. It's not that you take one, complete it and it is then discarded. No! Until you accomplish the first step, you cannot move on to the next step. There is no skipping around. God has given us an instruction manual to follow. If you try to skip just one step, you will abandon everything before it.

Step by Step

The first life principle we must have is "virtue." This means moral goodness. We have to set a moral standard in our lives of how we want to live. We need to draw lines in the sand and determine in our hearts that morally we will not go beyond that point. This is the first step because if you decide to live your life too loose and carefree, you will never carry the discipline you need to accomplish the second step – knowledge.

We add knowledge to a good moral standard. From where do you gain knowledge? The word "knowledge" here in the Greek is *gnōsis* which means "the deeper more perfect and enlarged knowledge of Christianity, such as belongs to the more advanced." You gain knowledge through the Word of God. It's only through His Word that you gain a deeper and more perfect knowledge of Christ.

Proverbs 3:5 teaches us not to lean on our own understanding. God wants us to stay in a constant state of dependency on Him. Don't allow yourself to get "too big for your britches" and convince yourself that you have obtained enough wisdom to make your own decisions. As you gain more knowledge of Christ through the Word of God, it will teach you our next great character trait – self-control.

One of my favorite scriptures in the Bible that I use frequently with the residents in our program is Proverbs 25:28, "Whoever has no self-control, is like a city broken down, without walls."

During the time of Solomon, cities built walls as a defense mechanism. If they had walls, they could place a watchman on the walls to sound an alarm if the enemy was approaching. Also, for the type of weapons being used, height gave an opponent a great advantage. So having walls allowed the men defending the city to stand on the top of the walls and it gave the men a better perspective.

So what God is conveying through this scripture is a person with no self-control over their life is a person that has no defense/walls against temptation or attacks. As you set a moral standard, gain knowledge through the Word of God, and build your walls of protection and self-control, you need to apply the following life principle – perseverance.

Persevering is continuing in a state of grace until it is succeeded by a state of glory. There is always a test before there is approval. I'm not referring to your acceptance in Christ. The moment you believe in Him, you are fully accepted and received into His Kingdom.

However, what I am referring to is how much God will entrust you with. So God will allow you to face a test for the purpose of proving you, and the one requirement for passing is persevering. Our Father knows that perseverance builds a determination within us to prove that faith in God will always prevail. Romans 5:3, 4, "And not only *that*, but we also glory in tribulations, knowing that tribulation produces perseverance; and perseverance, character; and character, hope."

The tribulation you might be facing, even now, is producing character traits within you to make you the greatest warrior you can possibly be for Christ. I know it's hard. I know it seems that you can't go on. But just remember that there are no great works done by strength, but rather by persevering. Christ is made strong in our weakness.

I love this Charles Spurgeon quote, "By perseverance the snail reached the ark." You will win in the end. Just keep on keeping on. Once you have added perseverance to your faith walk, you can now add your next life principle – respect.

By keeping your faith in God, no matter how hard life becomes, you learn that He will pull you through every ordeal. You will find the treasure of strength by holding onto His hand when you can't see your way. You learn that God cannot fail you, and as a result, you come to respect Him more and more. If I can show you something you fear, I can show you something you respect. That's why the fear/respect for God is the beginning of all wisdom. You will include God's wishes in every area of your life if you respect Him. You will carry a sense of desperation to know what He desires before you place your final stamp of approval on anything.

Isaiah 9:6 is a scripture I lean heavily on daily. And the key word within the scripture that brings me the most comfort is that Christ is our "Counselor." I also have the painting, "Divine Counselor" by Hollen, hanging on my wall.

Something I do each time I go to my office in the morning, I take the two chairs across from my desk and face them toward each other. I then kneel down in front of one and invite Jesus to come counsel me on every decision I have to make that day. I try my best, out of respect for God, to include Him in every aspect of my life. Why? I know that His way is the best way. I have tried it my way, and it doesn't work. I have also experienced enough hardship in my life to know that God is trustworthy.

Once you have added a high level of respect for God, then you can add your next life principle – brotherly kindness.

Love for those in our daily domain is an identifying mark by which the world can know we are disciples of Christ. When you add the grace of brotherly kindness, your relationship with God will keep compassion stirred in your heart for others. The Greek word for brotherly kindness is transliterated "Philadelphia," a compound involving two words: *phileo* (love) and *adelphos* (brother). It literally means "the love of brothers."

What the world notices most about us is the love we carry for one another. In a world filled with much hate, genuine love for our brother is especially observed among individuals who have been challenged in various social, economic, and racial backgrounds. If you attempt to be a witness for Christ, you will fail to appeal to those in the world unless there is a visible demonstration of true brotherly kindness. Once you have added brotherly kindness to your faith and are seeing more and more fruit being produced around you, it's time to add your final life principle in this passage – *agape* love.

Is there a perfect love? To answer this question, you cannot remain in the same thought pattern as the world. Watch the latest movie with a "love scene" in it and you will find what the world's concept of love is. There is a perfect love that comes from our Father, and it is *agapē*.

Before I attempt to explain *agapē* love, let's identify the other three categories of love in the Greek language.

The first category to look at is, s*torge* love. *Storge* is family affection. *Storge* means the love of a parent to a child and a child to the parent.

The next category of love is e*ros* love. Eros is the physical love and affection between a man and a woman. One interesting note is that the word erotic comes from the word *eros*. This is where the world has mixed up what God truly meant by love between a man and a woman, verses a perverted and selfishly driven relationship.

The next category of love is what we explored in the last paragraph, *phileo* love.

Lastly is *agape* love, which is generous and unselfish. *Agape* love is who God is and what He gives to us.

Examples of *agape* love are found in I Corinthians 13:4-7 "Love suffers long *and* is kind; love does not envy; love does not parade itself, is not puffed up; does not behave rudely, does not seek its own, is not provoked, thinks no evil; does not rejoice in iniquity, but rejoices in the truth; bears all things, believes all things, hopes all things, endures all things."

I have been asked several times if any human can achieve *agape* love for others. My response has always been, with man it is impossible, but through Christ all things are possible. And if we could not achieve *agape* love, then why would God instruct us to add it to our faith?

This doesn't mean that we won't ever make mistakes by saying or doing things we shouldn't. I'm confident we will all fall short at times, but we can add *agape* love to our faith and walk in it toward others, just as Christ did.

Run to Win the Race

Competition is what makes sports so attractive to

watch. And the more competitive a person you are, the more sports are involved in your life. The opposite is that normally noncompetitive people don't care to watch sports because it seems to be a waste of energy and time.

In the Kingdom of God, whether we are competitive or not, we are all in a race. Paul encourages us to run the race to obtain the prize. We should run our life race to obtain the Kingdom of God, which is our prize. Whether you enter four marathons every year or have never broken a sweat by even walking briskly, that doesn't matter. If you are a believer in Christ, you live in the Kingdom of God. Therefore, the moment Jesus entered into your heart, He said, "On your mark, get set..." the gun went off and the race began for you. Not only did Jesus enter you into this race, but He also destined you to win it!

As we run our race every day, we must stay prepared and healthy spiritually. By adding these seven life principles to your race, you will set your standard of achievement; have the knowledge you'll need to make the right calls; use self-control when being tempted to cheat, or overindulge; have the perseverance needed not to give up; let your respect for God motivate you; carry your torch of love for all those watching; and understanding God's love will ultimately bring you to the finish line victoriously, if you stay in the process.

Chapter Nine
Farm Market Road 449

On Friday, September 19th everyone returned home from vacation and seemed refreshed from a great time together. I had a good week of prayer and revelation and felt refreshed.

On Monday, I received a called from a man in our church named Randall. He fell on hard times and was requesting benevolence from the church to help with a few items. I knew him to be a great guy and faithful member so I started the process of getting him some finances.

When I called him back with an update on his request, he told me that he had a four-bedroom, two-baths mobile home on five acres that was empty and that he was trying to rent it for extra income. He also said it was on FM 449 outside the city limits.

The moment he told me, ringers began sounding in my spirit. It had enough rooms for our current needs and being that it was outside of the city, we had more liberty to house our men. So I told him the dilemma I was in with my men and asked if he would consider letting us rent it as another ministry home. He agreed so we immediately began making preparations to move most of our men to FM 449 and leave some at Fox Lane with Phil.

That night, James snuck out of the house and showed back up to Fox Lane drunk. While attempting to sneak back in, he began making a lot of noise and stumbling all over the living room. Trey heard the commotion and came out of his bedroom to investigate. When he saw what was going on, he pulled James outside to talk to him. They sat down on the front porch and Trey was trying to handle the situation without waking up Phil. As they were talking, James reached over and grabbed Trey in the crotch while he held his index finger to his mouth and said, "Shhhh."

Trey screams and falls off the steps trying to get away from him. Trey knew at this point that he was either going to hurt James very badly, or he needed to go wake up Phil. James was asked to leave that night.

The next day we took in a man named Chris Johnson. He would become a vital part of helping us make the next step. He was addicted to prescription pain killers and had ruined his relationship with his wife and son.

Although Trey had recently relapsed, he was trying his best to convince us and show us that he just made a mistake. He desperately wanted back into some type of leadership role. After everyone returned back from church service on Wednesday, Trey started pushing his point that he belonged in leadership with Phil. Phil is the most laid back and non-confrontational man I personally know. I had never seen him get upset about anything. But somehow this conversation with Trey began to get heated. Phil began telling Trey that he didn't need a title or a position, but the best way to lead was by setting the best example.

Jennifer calls me around 11 p.m. and says they had another problem. During the phone conversation, I hear

Trey's voiced raised and I thought I heard the phone drop.

Then Jennifer yells at Trey, "Stop pushing my husband."

I knew then what was happening so I hung up the phone and immediately left for Fox Lane. It was only a 10-minute drive and I filled every second of it with prayer. By the time I got there, Trey had already left with a girl who he called. I didn't know he even knew anyone that well in Longview.

Phil filled me in on what had transpired. I was very upset with Trey and couldn't understand how either of these men had allowed the conversation to get that far. I called Trey and told him to meet me at Whataburger by my house to discuss what happened. Being that Trey was a friend, I wanted to help him. Even to this day, I don't know if I have met anyone that has more potential than Trey.

We ordered some coffee and sat down to talk. I could tell right off the bat that I was getting nowhere with him. There was an excuse for all of his actions and remorse was thrown out the window long before we met. I told Trey that he couldn't go back to Fox Lane but evidently that didn't matter because he was already planning on staying with the girl.

As we were walking out of the restaurant, a local pastor named James Taylor drove up. He had a meeting at his church and it had run late. I don't believe Trey and James had ever met before, but as soon as James saw him he began to identify some troubled areas of Trey's life.

I was stunned. I began thinking, "How does he know all this about Trey without knowing him?" James even brought out parts of my conversation with Trey while talking a few minutes before. Trey fell under conviction knowing that the only way James could have known anything was by God revealing it to him.

The following morning during my devotions, I prayed about how to handle this situation. The Lord took me to Matthew 18 and reminded me of how to handle these matters. So I pulled Phil and Trey into the conference room at the church to resolve their differences and bring unity. Trey and Phil apologized to each other. Trey began to share from his heart which allowed us to get to the root cause of why the event took place. Trey was carrying jealousy and an expectation for favoritism from me because of our friendship. I stressed to him that those feelings didn't line up with the Word of God and that we were all on the same team, working towards the same goal of reaching the unreachable.

This was a God moment. The peace of God flooded that conference room and it was obvious that God had moved on Trey's heart. I didn't want to let Trey back in immediately because there were still consequences for his actions. Our policy stated that he would have to stay out for seven days for his actions.

Final Straw

On September 27th, Trey moved into FM 449 with six other residents. Four residents stayed at Fox Lane with Phil and Jennifer. FM 449 was an empty home with only a couch, a cot, two beds and one mattress. But we were all content and grateful that God had opened this door.

During our move, we took in a new guy who came to us for help. His name was Waylan. Waylan was in his early twenties, very short, with a muscular build and had a bad case of small-man syndrome. He had come in at a bad time for us because we were in the middle of transitioning into our new home, so we never administered a drug test to see if he needed detoxing before entering our program.

The first night in our new home, Waylan started hallucinating about demons coming after him. In the middle of the night, he flopped out of his bed and ran into the kitchen to grab a knife. He then ran to the other side of the house, pushed open the bedroom door where Trey was sleeping and, with a knife in his hand, hopped in the bed with Trey asking him to protect him.

Trey jumped out of his bed, flipped the light on and hollered, "What are you doing?!"

"Protect me! They were trying to get me in my room," Waylan said.

"Who's trying to get you? And where did you get that knife?" Trey asked.

Visibly shaken, Waylan said, "The demons! They were running for me! Please, protect me. I'm scared."

Trey thought about the perception of having another man in the program sleeping beside him, but he put those feelings aside for the night. He took the knife away from Waylan and put it back in the kitchen. Trey then moved to one side of the bed and let Waylan sleep on the other.

We were still getting calls and having men come to us daily needing help. But we didn't have the beds to sleep anyone else and really didn't want to put our men on the floor. A few days later Chris, one of our residents, suggested that we call a guy at a local mission. Chris had stayed there before and was aware of many bunk beds that they had stored away.

Phil tells him to call. The local mission director told us to get as many as we needed. We took 20 beds, all they had. We knew this was God once again supplying our needs. The next weekend we took in three more men, Billy, Milford and Mickey.

Part of the verse the Lord gave me in Luke 5:4 said that the disciples had caught so many fish that they called on their partner boats for help. As I saw our ship getting full, I knew that we needed to start calling on our partner ministries for help. We began planning a community meeting with local pastors and businessmen to make them aware of the vision that God had given us. We planned it for Tuesday, September 30th at mid-day. Out of the 25 we invited, only ten were able to make it. We asked a few of our current residents James, Jimmy and Trey to speak. Each man shared from their heart and it went great.

During the meeting, one pastor told me that his church will commit to $1,000 a month. Two other businessmen stated that they would commit to $500 a month.

Another businessman asked if we had a big need he could help with. I had printed out a paper listing all of our needs on it and on the top of the page was a passenger van. I referred him to the list and he said that he would purchase us the van. Another man that was present took off his hat and suggested they take up an offering for our guys to have a barbecue that night. They passed the hat and collected $176.

Being new to all of this and really just flying by the seat of my pants, I was amazed by the response we received. I began thinking that we needed to do a community awareness meeting every month.

Put My Hand in the Hand of Man

I learned a valuable lesson through this first meeting. I could tell that over the next few days all I could think about was how to get in front of more affluent people who had the finances to underwrite our ministry. My focus had shifted because of the wonderful results we saw during our first meeting. I began looking to man as my resource rather than God.

God had instructed me years before never to ask "man" for finances, but always pray to Him when I was in time of need. I was turning from my conviction. My actions did not take God by surprise. God knew that instead of putting my hand in His hand to follow Him, I was trying to put my hand in the hands of man.

So what happened? None of the commitments that were made ever came through. Although I believe these men had good intentions, not one of them followed through with their word. We did end up with a 15-passenger van being donated to us, but it was from someone who did not attend that meeting. And the $176 dollars that was taken up in the hat for our men's dinner that night never made it into our hands.

After the meeting was over, the man wanted his hat back so he took the money out and gave it to Trey. We had already prearranged for Trey to leave with his parents after the meeting. The plan was for Trey to stay with them until after dinner. Then they were to drop him back off at our house. Trey left with his parents and they went back to their hotel room. After a couple of hours there, Trey told them he was stepping outside for a little while but never returned.

His parents called me later to inform me of the situation. The next morning around 6 a.m. I get a call from Chris asking where the van and Trey were. We knew that Trey had left but where did our van go? I began to think that Trey might have found his way back to FM 449 and taken our van. So I tried calling a few places where I thought Trey might be but couldn't get hold of him. A couple of hours later, Chris called and said that Trey just showed up, but was in a different car. Now I don't know what is going on. Chris also said that it was obvious Trey was high.

I got in my truck and headed that way. Trey was already gone again by the time I got there. Trey's parents called later and said he had showed up at the hotel. So I asked to speak with him. I informed Trey that he was out of the program and that I only wanted to see him again when he was truly ready for change.

The next day, Trey showed up at the church with one of the businessmen who attended our meeting the day before. Somehow he had convinced this man that we were falsely accusing him. Out of respect for this man, I invited both of them to come to my office. Trey denied everything. However I would not relent. I knew that Trey was behind our van being gone. I knew that Trey had taken the money and relapsed with it. I stayed persistent with Trey and kept catching him in his lies. It didn't take very long before Trey admitted to his wrongs and accepted the consequences for his actions.

Enabling

There is a hot topic among those who have someone

they know who's addicted to a controlling substance and/or alcohol. It's called "enabling." When you see a homeless man on the side of the road with a sign saying, "Need food. Please help" what do you do? Do you give him or her money, believing in the back of your mind that it will be used for their addictions? Do you roll up your window and act as though you never saw them, and just keep on going about your merry way?

When you have a loved one that you know is addicted to drugs, yet they call you with an incredibly sad story of how they are hungry, nowhere to turn, no one to turn to, what do you do? Do you run to help them every time? Do you leave them in their mess in hopes that one day they will show up at your house in a suit and tie, totally clean and off their habits?

These are hard choices to make, especially when you love the person. But this is the battle families across our land face on a daily basis. Where should we draw the line and stop offering help? I get asked this question a lot, primarily by parents. Here are my thoughts on when to lean toward grace and rescue a person out of their mess, and when to leave them in it.

In the ministry of recovery, what we look for the most is whether the person is truly looking for change or is truly looking to be enabled to continue in the addiction. Each one of us has to be extremely careful not to give in to their constant requests. It takes great caution not to fund their habit of drinking or using.

Paying for a cell phone, paying rent, bailing out of jail or hiring a lawyer are all prime examples of enabling the person. You might be asking, "How is paying a person's rent enabling them to further their addiction?" Maybe the better questions to ask are, "Why is this person not able to pay for his own rent? Where are his finances going?"

The majority of people living on the streets are not just down on their luck or have fallen on hard times. Most agencies that have done research on this subject place the percentage of people who are homeless, due to an addiction, at over 80 percent. The average percentage of the homeless with mental illnesses is 17 percent. And of the 17 percent with this condition, 11 percent have mental illness due the years of drug abuse.

Only three percent are truly seeking help for the sake of their well being. So a high percentage of people who are homeless are in that condition because that is the most economical way to live and still feed their addiction. They would rather use their choice of drugs than have a roof over their head. They would rather have that "40" in their hands than have a healthy meal in front of them.

Please don't misunderstand what I'm communicating. We are talking about enabling them to remain in their condition. I'm not talking about whether they want to be there or not. I honestly believe that most of the people struggling with an addiction truly want change deep inside. They are trying to cope with their shame, guilt, abuse and other issues of the past. They don't know how to find the healing they need. They don't know how to break that bondage of addiction in their lives. Most have been in and out of rehab and have finally settled in their hearts that there is no hope. There is no question in my heart that they feel trapped. And this is precisely why we have to be very careful not to enable or rescue them unless they are ready for change.

So how do you know when to reach out your hand to

grab the one sinking in front of you?

First of all, you must allow the Holy Spirit to lead you. You cannot trust your own wisdom or feelings. They will misguide you every time. Spend time praying to the Father. He loves that person more than you will ever love them. He knows that person better than you will ever know them. Even if they are a son or daughter, they are still only a gift to you. God is their creator. God knows the answer and He will use you to reach them if you will remove yourself or get out of His way and allow Him to break them.

Psalm 51:17 teaches us that it is a broken heart that God seeks in each one of us. Allow God to bring them to the place of brokenness that He desires for their life. I know this is very hard. I know it will take every fiber of your being to say "no." But any other answer than that, you are playing god in their life. You are trying to supply all their needs according to your riches and glory, rather than His. You are not allowing them to experience God and His faithfulness to them. It's the broken that God can change, mold and make into the vessels of honor He has created them to be.

Secondly, I have found that it's time to intervene when the individual is willing to do whatever is required of them. The best phone calls I receive from those wanting help are the ones that never ask what the rules are. They just want in. The ones I worry about are the ones that have to know every little thing they can get away with. And once in the program, the ones I give the best chance of making it are those who comply with the guidelines and rules we have set in place.

If your loved one comes to you and says, "I want help, but before I can get it, please give me $20 for gas.

My car is stuck on the side of the road."

At that moment, please let the largest red flag your mind can imagine wave in your head. It's not gas they want. The conversation you are looking for is, "I want help! I don't care where I go, how long I have to be there or when they can get me in. I just want help." That's the desperation for God that will loose the bonds of oppression over an individual's life.

Thirdly, you will know it's time by how grateful they are for your help. I'm convinced that when the rubber meets the road, it's not drugs they are truly addicted to. It's not alcohol they keep running back to. The number one thing they are addicted to is self. The root of using drugs and alcohol is selfishness. They don't care who it hurts. They don't care who they are robbing from. They don't care about anybody but themselves.

Recently, a man who had been in our program long enough to receive a pass, exercised his privilege and went home for Christmas. I remember his family being so excited that we approved his pass. His wife even had their two girls call and express how grateful they were that we would let them see their daddy for Christmas. His first day back he and his wife went Christmas shopping for their two young girls. She had saved up all she could for the girls and had planned on spending all she had on them. She wanted the girls to know that daddy loved them so she also waited until he returned so the girls would know that daddy was part of buying them gifts.

When they got back home, he told his wife that he was stepping outside for some fresh air. Instead, he went through her purse and got the keys to her car. He then took all $600 worth of toys to a nearby pawn shop. He pawned off all the toys and headed to the closest crack house where he spent every penny relapsing. He didn't care that he left his own children with no presents. He didn't care that his wife had worked very hard to save up and had nothing left in her account. He didn't care that all his kids really wanted for Christmas was their dad to be home and well. He could only think about himself and what he wanted.

Now this is a man who had been clean for nine months. His detoxing was done. All chemicals previously in his body are all flushed out by now. So if it is not selfishness driving a man to pull a stunt like that, you tell me what else it is! Plus, that is one true story out of hundreds more I could share.

If you want to help someone, don't enable them. Allow them to come to the end of themselves. Let them hit bottom. Cover them in prayer and God will protect them. Once you have acknowledged Him in their lives, move out of His way and trust in Him with all your heart. He knows what he is doing.

Under New Management

It was enabling that drove this businessman to ask us to consider just putting Trey on a probation period and to keep him in leadership. I tried to explain to him that Trey couldn't be trusted because he had just relapsed two weeks earlier. But he could not fathom asking Trey to leave. He let me know that he did not approve of my decision and he put Trey up in a cabin he owned.

I went back to our recovery home, pulled all the men together and told them that Trey had relapsed and that's why he would no longer be around. I worked on a new schedule for the program. I assigned Chris as a residential leader to bring more structure. And I began rotating out on staying the night out at FM 449 with the men to have a leader in place at all times. I picked up the emotional pieces I had for Trey and continued moving forward with the ministry.

A few weeks passed and everything was running pretty smooth. One evening Chris came to me and expressed how God was doing some great things in his marriage. He was seeing that the more he surrendered and trusted his life to God, the more his life and marriage were being restored. He said that he and his wife were talking about getting back together and trying to work on their marriage.

Misty and I sat down to visit with her and I was impressed by how she was handling the situation and the grace she was giving. We began to allow her to visit Chris more while offering more counseling to them. I then allowed Chris to take a pass one weekend to spend the weekend with her. I was seeing Chris make long strides in his recovery and relationship with God. I decided to give him more responsibility. I let him lead the evening Bible studies so that we didn't have to stay the night away from our families anymore. I gave this some time and just monitored everything.

Chris approached me after some time and asked if his wife and son could move into the master bedroom. He said that he wanted to take the next step up in leadership and toward his marriage. At first I wasn't sure about it but, after praying, I had a peace that this could benefit him and our ministry.

So she moved in and it was awesome seeing this young family take on such a vital role in our recovery program. Chris and his wife led our Monday evening teaching, house meetings on Tuesday nights and our chapel service on Thursday nights. During this time, Chris also continued coming to me with some great ideas for the program and I knew in my heart that in time, Chris could become our next program director.

He's Back in Black

I've always believed that it is important to keep your perspective large about life and ministry. I take mission trips and attend conferences for two reasons. First, I go to learn, grow and serve in any capacity I can. Second, I go because it allows me to see ministry from a different angle. So when Chris told me about a program within driving distance, I jumped at the chance to gain a new perspective on recovery ministry. Chris and I loaded up and headed that way excited about the insight we were sure we would receive.

While there, I get a phone call from the businessman who took Trey with him from our meeting.

He asked, "Have you heard from Trey?"

"Nope. The last time I saw or spoke to him was when he left our meeting with you," I replied.

He went on to tell me that he had some brand new trucks that a customer ordered and he gave Trey permission to demo one. However, Trey has not returned in the truck for two days. He then said that if Trey did not return the truck by that evening, which was the day it had to be delivered, he was going to report it as stolen and press charges.

I told him I was sorry that this had occurred and if I should hear from Trey I would be sure to let him know.

Then I went on with our tour.

A couple of hours later, Trey called him. Trey was at Lake of the Pines, out of gas and out of money.

On my way back home I get a call from this man again. "Tim, I'm sorry to bother you, but I'm at a loss here. I don't know what to do with Trey. Is there any way you can help?"

I agreed and when we returned from our trip, I went out to meet Trey. He had relapsed again. I got the truck back to the man and he kicked Trey out of the cabin he had been living in. I took advantage of this opportunity to make another attempt to get Trey to come back into our program. Trey would not even consider it. He just asked to be dropped off by a local mission. Trey was back out on the streets, homeless and seemed to be worse off than what he was before.

I started getting phone calls from businesses saying that there was a man there claiming to be associated with my church and that he was the program director for House of Disciples. Each one of them said that he was asking for cash donations. I knew it was Trey on the streets panhandling for money to feed his addiction so I would always correct the information quickly. This went on for awhile.

One Wednesday evening after service, a young lady in the church approached Misty and me and said that she needed to tell us something about Trey. She had a concerned look on her face so we paused and sat in the foyer of our church to hear what she had to say.

She began by telling us that she knew she had messed up and that she was fearful of him. She said that she had seen a man walking on the side of the road one night in the rain. She recognized him as Trey from the church so she stopped to ask him if he needed a ride. She was not aware of the relapses and other offenses Trey had committed recently, so she took him in. Trey convinced her that he had nowhere to sleep. It was cold and raining and he was not feeling well. So she brought him home with her believing she was helping a church member out.

She went on to explain how after a couple of days of staying there, Trey convinced her that he needed a bus ticket back to Austin, some clothes and money to eat for his trip. She explained to him that she didn't have the money, but he would not take no for an answer. And he said that he had a truck in Austin and that he was going to sell to pay her back once he got there. She ended up taking a small loan out on her car to give him the cash to get what he wanted.

He took the money and left his belongings at her house. He was gone a couple of days but returned without the money, without any clothes, and without a bus ticket. She began to cry and say that she had done something horribly wrong, too. She said that he began making advances at her and finally she let her guard down and had sex with him. She said that she felt trapped and was very fearful of what might happen next.

I tried to give her the best advice I could, which was to turn and run far away from him as she could. When she returned to her apartment that night, Trey was gone. She took all his belongings and sat them outside her door and locked it. He showed back up around 3 a.m. banging on the door. She saw him through the door but just told him to go away.

At 4 a.m., I wake up hearing someone outside my

window calling my name. It was cool outside so I left our window open. I immediately recognize the voice. I began to think that she must have told him what I said and he was coming over to start some trouble.

I leaned over to the window and I could see a car with it's lights on in my driveway. I get up and go to my back door to meet him, really not knowing what to expect. Trey had a taxi bring him over to my house and drop him off. He had all of his stuff in four trash bags. I asked him what he needed and he said that he had contacted a recovery home and they accepted him. He said that he didn't have enough money to have the taxi take him over so he wanted to know if I would take him.

I invited him in and told him I wanted to verify his story. I called the recovery home and they said they had spoken to Trey and had a bed open for him. I told Trey to load up his stuff in my car and I would get dressed to take him. As we started on our way there Trey began talking crazy. It was as though he was bragging about all the stuff that he had been doing.

I ask him to please not talk about it because it was offensive and it seemed that he was proud of his actions. My request only made it worse, but I just kept driving. He then went on to tell me about how he took advantage of this girl by getting her to try a substance and having sex with her.

As he followed the statement by laughing, I slammed on my brakes and pulled over to the side of the road.

"Trey, either you shut your mouth right now and don't say a word the rest of this trip, or you can start walking from here," I said, while leaning over to his seat and looking him straight in the eyes. "Don't you realize how much you hurt people when you mistreat them?

Don't you even care about anyone's feelings but yours?"

"Alright! Alright! Alright! I'll just keep it to myself," he said with a smirk on his face.

I was fuming, but I tried to focus on getting him to the recovery program.

We rode in silence for a short time then Trey asked, "Did I tell you that she was a virgin?"

I jerked the car into the parking lot of a convenience store, got out and started pulling Trey's bags out of the car.

As I'm doing this, Trey gets out and walks around to my side with his hands in a fist hollering, "You think you are going to kick me out of your car, boy? Is that what you think?"

At first I turned toward him preparing to fight. When I saw that he was just standing there barking at me, I shut the door, took the keys out of my ignition and walked into the store. I told the clerk to call the police.

"What for," she asked.

Will you please call the police!" I quickly replied.

About that time, Trey had followed me into the store. He walked right up to my face and began cursing and calling me a few choice names not suitable to mention in this book. I didn't know what to think about the situation. I wasn't sure if I was about to get killed by Trey or if someone would intervene, I was just praying. Only by the grace and protection of God, Trey turned and walked outside. I saw him ask a guy for a cigarette and began smoking right by the front door. I just stood there by the counter.

I'm sure the police officers were there in a matter of minutes, but it felt like forever. One talked to Trey outside and the other came in to talk to me. I began to explain what happened to the police officer and that I just wanted to get the rest of Trey's stuff out of my car and go home.

The police officer's response floored me. "Listen, Sir. It's 5:30 in the morning. I don't have time to answer calls because two lovers decide to break up."

I was at a loss for words, but somehow managed to say, "A lover's quarrel? That's what you think this is? NO! I'm a married man."

Feeling like I wasn't getting anywhere with this policeman, I began walking out to my car to leave. Trey began coming behind shouting, "What do you think you're doin,' boy?"

The other police officer gets Trey to stop and he walks out with me to my car. This time I decided to use more detail to explain the events so there wouldn't be any more confusion. I could tell immediately the change in his reaction. He called over the other policeman and explained. They then told me to get his stuff out and leave.

While I'm pulling Trey's stuff out of my car, I could hear him making remarks. Both of the policemen walked up to Trey and dealt with him forcefully. As that is going on, I jump in my car, totally relieved and leave for home. I remember my nerves being in high alert and I was shaking while holding on to the steering wheel driving.

I'll never forget that moment. As I reflect back, I now realize all the mistakes I made in putting myself in a vulnerable situation. As I shared earlier, there are times when you reach out to someone in need. There are other times when you are enabling someone. This was a classic story of enabling. Because I loved Trey as a brother being that we grew up together, I let my heart get the better of me. I could have avoided a lot of unnecessary stress during these circumstances had I not entered into an enabling mode. Some of you are experiencing a lot of stress while dealing with someone addicted. Save yourself. Until someone comes to you ready for change, as hard as it is, don't enable them.

The best way I can describe Trey's action is like a tornado. He came to town, tore up everything in his path and left everyone else to pick up the pieces behind him. The unfortunate part of it all is that it appeared he was never remorseful over any of his actions.

I did find out later that somehow he found his way to the program I was taking him to. He stayed for one month, got into an altercation with their leadership and was asked to leave. After a couple of years, Trey called wanting to come into our program. He had been living on the streets in Austin and was desperate for help.

Today, Trey is in our program working on his recovery. Just as God is a God of multiple chances, so we must be willing to give multiple chances to those who are ready for change. Trey has the potential to be a great leader and we hope – and are willing to work hard – to channel his leadership in God's direction. I believe this time is the right time for Trey.

Most of the drama lessened as we grew in knowledge on how to run a program. We began to implement more guidelines as we saw fit. We continued giving Chris more responsibilities and began training him to be the program director.

We raised Milford and Mickey into residential leadership roles. We also placed Mickey over coordinating transportation for work, doctor appointments, parole appointments, etc. We implemented phases and began using Fox Lane as a home for our upper phase guys. Everything began to come together and get organized.

We were beginning to see more fruit for our labor and God's favor remained on our efforts. Our number of men would fluctuate, but we stayed at a steady rate of climb. We believed that God was entrusting us with more of His sheep to shepherd and we were giving it our very best!

Chapter Ten
Marriage For Dummies

In September of 2008, I got a call from Ruby. She is one of the ladies we picked up at our second Party in the Park and dropped off at the hotel. Ruby had been arrested numerous times for prostitution. She also had an addiction to drugs. She called me from the hospital. She had been beat up by a "john" trying to pick her up for a trick. She told me that she was tired of this lifestyle and living on the streets. She asked me to help her pull out of her mess.

At the time, we didn't have a home for women, but I was willing to do all I could to get her some help. I called Caryn and she dropped everything to go to the hospital to pick her up and take her to her home. Caryn often opened her own home to help women who lived on the streets. Caryn has a huge heart for helping women and she has always been a great inspiration to anyone around her.

Ruby sobered up and stopped prostituting herself. Some of her regular clients called, but Ruby stuck to her guns and cut them off, also. Her drug of choice was cocaine, but she also had to spend some time coming off pain killers and muscle relaxers.

Ruby and Eric had formed a relationship on the streets. They knew each other's lifestyles and it was acceptable to them. I know that might be hard to believe for some, but it is a completely different world on the streets. What is abnormal to you and me is totally embraced when you are hooked on drugs and homeless.

Ruby began opening up to us after she found that we were just here to help and not condemn. She told us a story during one of our group sessions of what she went through while trying to survive the streets and feed her additions. She told us how one evening a "john" picked up her and asked if she would go home with him for the evening instead of getting a cheap room or turning the a trick in the truck.

She agreed and then the nightmare began. When they arrived at his trailer house, he invited her in. Once inside the front door, he hit her in the back of the head, knocking her out cold. When she woke up, she was tied to a bed, totally naked. She spent the next six days tied up, repeatedly raped and relied upon this man to feed, bathe and accompany her to the restroom.

She reported it to the police but because they knew her as a prostitute, she said they just accused her of not getting paid for the trick and wanted revenge. It was during times like those that she said Eric was always there for her. And the more she got involved with Eric, the more she felt protected and secure.

A few weeks passed and Ruby was making strides for recovery and in her relationship with God. Ruby told Eric that she loved him, but she couldn't live that way anymore. After a few weeks, Eric called on a Saturday morning letting us know that he wanted help. We took him in and began the process of recovery. He quit drinking and began reading the Bible on a regular basis. Both Eric and Ruby were excited about changing their lives.

They knew the direction they were going would bring lasting joy and happiness, unlike the temporary counterfeit the streets offered.

During the time that Eric and Ruby were with us, our pastor began teaching a series on marriage entitled Marriage for Dummies. He announced that at the end of the series he was going to conduct a ceremony for each couple in the church to renew their vows if they wanted.

That announcement struck a nerve with Eric. He had been reading his Bible daily and drawing close to God. During one of his morning devotions, he learned that in order for him and Ruby to be living together again, and be in right standing with the Word, they needed to get married.

Eric asked Ruby to marry him the week before the teaching began so they could attend every series. She accepted, but on one condition. She wanted to make sure Eric was planning on sticking to his recovery and not drop out of the program. Eric promised Ruby that if he dropped out, the marriage was off.

I spoke with the pastor about them getting married and he agreed to sign their license. A friend gave Ruby her wedding dress. Another lady gave her some shoes and jewelry to wear during the service. A beautician from the church offered to do her hair and make-up. A few of us pitched in to get Eric a nice suit to wear as well. It was coming together nicely.

The Sunday before Thanksgiving was the big day! Eric was beside himself with excitement. We had a photographer lined up to come to take pictures of all the couples in the ceremony, but we gave her a little extra to focus on Ruby and Eric.

It was a special event for me because I was seeing

how our program was helping to restore a family. After the ceremony, the couples that participated had a reception at a nice restaurant downtown. We had the photographer take several pictures at the reception of them cutting the cake. We put a lot of effort into finding Eric's family to send them an invitation. We did not know if they would attend, but we thought it would be worth the try.

Ruby told us that she had no one to contact. We tried to research it anyway, but came up with nothing. As sad as it seemed, Ruby was all by herself. Several of Eric's family members showed up. His mom, sisters and his very handsome 12-year-old son. While visiting with them, we learned that Eric came from a very wealthy family. We also learned that he was also a successful upholster. Also, Eric was in the military for many years.

We took many pictures of everyone together. Eric and Ruby felt on top of the world. We planned for them to move into Fox Lane together after they got married. We set up their own bedroom and tried to make everything as comfortable as we could for them.

The Little Foxes on Fox Lane

Ruby got a job taking care of an elderly man in an apartment complex across town. Eric went back to work for a former employer doing upholstering. Everything was going fine, so we thought. Our inexperience with addictions once again got the best of us.

Phil and Jennifer were still our house parents on Fox Lane at the time. Phil began to grow suspicious of how much Nyquil Jimmy would drink on a daily basis. Phil did not realize that he had just replaced an actual beer for as much Nyquil as he could drink.

Jimmy knew that we wouldn't think too much about something we use at times. So still observing but oblivious to what was happening all around them, Phil and Jennifer decided to take a weekend trip with the residents. Jennifer's parents lived on a huge lake so they decided to take everyone there for fishing, camping out and grilling. Phil allowed Ruby to stay back to "take care of" her client.

During the trip, Phil noticed that Eric and Jimmy were constantly at odds with each other. What Phil didn't know was that Jimmy was getting upset with Eric for not sharing some valium he had got from Ruby. Jimmy decided he would take matters into his own hands. He claimed to Phil that his allergies were acting up. So when Phil pulled down a medicine box which held all of Jennifer's mom's medications, Jimmy saw the soma and came back later to take them all. Phil noticed that while everyone else was out having a good time, all Jimmy wanted to do was sleep.

Jennifer decided to get involved to see what she could find out about this bizarre behavior. She asked Jimmy what kind of allergy pills he was taking. When jimmy pulled out the empty bottle, she knew what happened. Jimmy and Eric ended up sleeping the whole weekend and did not participant in any activities.

When they got back to Longview, Phil launched an investigation. After spending hours interviewing everyone, he finally cracked their code of silence and found the holes in our program. He learned that the man who Ruby was working for was supplying her pain pills. Ruby knew that a pain pill on the streets was worth five to 10 dollars. So she would sell the pills then purchase cocaine and sneak it back into the house. Before Phil knew it, everyone on Fox lane had relapsed. They would literally sit on the back porch and smoke crack while Phil and Jennifer would be in their bedroom.

Ruby started calling in stating that she had to stay over night to help this man with his meds, etc. What she was actually doing was going back out to the streets and trying to turn tricks. She once again fell deep into her craving for cocaine. One of our residents confessed that Ruby had given him and the others crack. Phil called a house meeting to bring everyone together and make them aware of his findings and that their actions would not be tolerated.

Phil also found many pornographic magazines stashed away in each bedroom. Evidently, the magazines were found in the trash during one of our community work days where our residents go out to help families move, pick up their yard or anything else we could do to serve them.

That same day, Ruby came home and Phil confronted her. She denied everything, but it was obvious by the way she looked. She had not bathed in days and her speech was slurred. Phil called making me aware of his findings so we could put our heads together.

My heart went out to everyone there. I didn't feel right about kicking them all back out on the streets, but I also knew that we could not allow everything to continue on without some type of recourse. We thought the best way to handle it was to cut off the source, Ruby's job. So we sat Eric and Ruby down and asked them both not to continue working, but to focus on their recovery. We explained that we would make up the difference financially.

Eric was willing to do whatever we asked of him. He truly wanted to change, but Ruby would not consider any offer we made. We tried and tried to convince Ruby to let us help her, but the more we spoke, the more determined she was to continue in her lifestyle.

Knowing that she was not going to budge, I had to ask them to leave. They packed up their belongings and walked out. They had nowhere to go but to the streets. I cannot ever remember a time of being more devastated. The saddest part to me was that Eric truly wanted help, but he felt he had no choice but to be there for his wife.

Before confronting Jimmy with his terms, Phil found him in his bedroom crying. Jimmy explained that he had more to confess. He had also stolen a nail gun from Phil and pawned it to buy crack. One glimmer of hope that we saw in Jimmy was that his emotions came from how low he had gotten, not because he got caught.

"I can't believe that my addictions are driving me to steal from and hurt the very people trying to help me. It's like I can't stop. It's like I have no control over my actions," he said.

This was the perfect position for Jimmy to be in because up to this point, he was trying to stop on his own. But he now realized that it is only through the help and grace of God. We shared with Jimmy that all his privileges were taken away and that he would need to move out to our FM 449 location so he could receive my accountability.

Another role I had to play in this was ministering to Phil. He felt horrible and very embarrassed about everyone failing. He also felt like he had failed as a leader and that this was more his fault than even the residents. It gave me the opportunity to share a valuable principle I had to learn early on in ministry.

I said, "Phil, keep your chin up. We are responsible to people, but not for people. Our job is to love and care for the needs of those God has entrusted to us. But whether they receive and respond is out of our control."

Phil adopted this truth and began handling situations like this with a more grace perspective.

A Miracle on Green Street

Since Fox Lane had all but cleared out due to everyone relapsing, it gave me the opportunity to take a closer look at our operation and what we could do to save on expenses. At this time, Misty and I were still funding all our efforts. God always supplied, but we ran a very tight budget that left no room in our bank account for any large or unexpected expense. We were currently paying rent, utilities and other maintenance items on two locations that only gave us a little over 3,000 square feet of living area. Plus, by the time we added up what our bills ran for these two locations, I figured that we could get more living space, which would allow us to reach more men and still not pay as much on total expenses. So we began discussing and researching property around the Longview area that could house all our men.

During this time, we met a man named Johnny Collier. He invited us to minister at a Tri-Fest event he was hosting. Johnny served on the board for two other ministries for homeless men and women called New Gate and 12 Way Foundation. Johnny struggled with an addiction to drugs and alcohol in his life and had compassion for others in the same condition.

At the event, many of the unsheltered came out. The

gym was packed and everyone ate a hot meal and heard some wonderful testimonies of God's love. We didn't spend much time talking to Johnny at the event because we all stayed busy setting up equipment and preparing to minister in song.

About a week passed by and Johnny stopped by my office unexpectedly to visit with me. He brought brochures of the other ministries he was involved with and expressed that he wanted to network with other ministries reaching the same people. He shared with me that "we are stronger working together than apart."

The whole time he was talking, I felt impressed by the Holy Spirit to plant a seed into these ministries. So after sharing his story and how wonderful these ministries are, he stood up to leave but I asked him to wait. I pulled out my check book and wrote a check for a thousand dollars.

Johnny said, "Hey man, I didn't come here to get any money from you."

"I understand, but I have to be obedient to what the Lord has laid on my heart to do."

He seemed very puzzled by this, especially since we were just starting out ourselves. But at the time he and I both understood that there is a valuable principle in what the Lord asked me to do. It's the law of sowing and reaping. By sowing into those ministries and helping them fulfill their dreams, God would bring a harvest into our ministry to fulfill the dreams He gave us.

The following week, Johnny invited me to go with him to one of the ministry locations and take a tour. It was very insightful to see the inner workings of this ministry and how it operated. I remember walking around in awe and hoping one day that God would trust us with helping as many people.

The director took time away from his daily duties and shared with us how they got started. I heard marvelous stories of how God blessed them and all the miracles that God performed. After a few hours there, we began our journey home. I sat in the back seat and just stared out the window. It felt as if God had given me a glimpse of where He was taking us. I was more motivated than ever before.

The next few weeks God began to give me new visions and directions for our ministry. I received a vision for starting ministry centers all across the nation. God showed me that these centers would have church services for the men in our program. He showed me that our discipleship program, a new food and clothing ministry would all be part of His plans for these centers. God was matching every item Jesus mentioned in Matthew 25 and Isaiah 58 to our mission.

As the New Year rolled around, we began actively seeking a place to purchase for the ministry to expand. It seemed that every place we drove by that was for sale, I was trying to see if that was the land we were to possess. We saw a couple of properties that looked promising. One was a nursing home and the other an apartment complex.

During our search, my parents drove by an old funeral home that was located downtown. It was beautiful and it fit the vision for ministry centers perfectly. It was built in 1937 and was colonial in style, with four huge columns in the front, white with a circle drive and green shutters. The square footage was 12,000. It had living quarter's upstairs, administrative offices and a marvelous chapel.

The first time I saw it, I just knew this was the building we were to expand into. It was going to be a huge step of faith to buy the building because not only did we not have the money for the down payment, we didn't know if we could afford the payments if we did move forward with the purchase. But there are times when you just know that God is leading you to stretch your faith. This was one of those times for us.

After praying multiple times about this potential property, I continued hearing a number in my head – $250,000. The original asking price was $600,000, but owners had recently come down to $400,000. I asked the Lord to make His will clearly known to us. So my fleece before Him was that if we could get the building for $250,000 or less, I would know that it was not just my emotions getting the best of me, but rather His divine will.

I called the broker to get all the information I could about the building. I started calling him so much to go see it that the realtor gave me his key so I would stop bugging him. I showed it to Johnny, he and my dad encouraged me to make an offer of $205,000 to get the bidding started and see where the owners were at.

When I called the broker about our offer, he said with a chuckle, "Tim, they have recently remodeled the whole building. Not to mention, they even paid much more than that when they bought it. I'm sorry, but we won't entertain that offer."

I pleaded with him, "Please, just send in the offer and let's see what happens. I believe we are supposed to have this building, but I have to start here. Please!"

After a long pause, he replied, "Alright, but just so you know, they probably won't bother to counter. They turned down $305,000 a few months ago."

I drove to his office, we put up $500 in earnest money and continued praying. A few days went by and I had not heard anything. My first thought was that the offer was so insulting that even the realtor didn't want to bother me with a reply. But I thought I would call to check, anyway. The realtor said that the owners never replied to the email he sent. He said that he would call to make sure that received it.

Later that day he calls me, "I'm a little taken back, Tim. They want to counter your offer at $300,000."

Surprised and filled with excitement, all I could say was, "Really?"

We countered back at $225,000.

A few days passed and the realtor called back. "They took a few days to consider your offer and they decided to bring their final to the table. It is a take it or, leave it deal."

With great anticipation I asked, "Ok. What is their final offer?"

"Two-hundred-forty-two thousand dollars," he said.

I stood up and with a giant leap of faith said, "We'll take it!"

If What You Have is Not Enough, Plant a Seed

In recent years, we have heard many preachers using modern media to amplify some incorrect views of God. I have seen them stake their claim on one passage of scripture, making a strong argument in hopes that the viewer will throw money at the preacher's cause. The Bible clearly states that we should not judge another, however it does allow for us to judge one's fruit. And it seems that the fruit or motivation behind the actions of these preachers is not to disciple or grow one's knowledge of the Word of God. Instead, the fruit I often saw displayed was a pursuit for finances.

For example, I remember watching a video of a preacher claiming that if you send him a certain amount of money, he would add you to his prayer list and send you a cloth that carries supernatural power. I have never understood this because the power is not in the cloth, but in the God who made the cloth. And we have access to His supernatural power day or night, with or without that cloth. And the fact that the TV preacher would only send it to you based on you first sending him money really bothered me.

I share this because I want to touch on sowing and reaping, but I don't want you to tie my thoughts on this subject to another preacher wanting money. The motivation behind this chapter is to share my personal experiences and my beliefs. However, I'm not trying to make a religion out of my beliefs or share this in a way that will cause you to give to me. I'm sharing this because it is part of the story.

Settling on the price for the building was only the first step. Now we had to come up with the down payment and the finances. I went to several banks and each one of them declined to finance us.

They told me, "You are too new of an organization."

I also heard, "You don't have any financial history."

And I heard, "You have no guarantor that will make sure that we will get paid."

It was the same response everywhere I went. I knew that God wanted us to have this building but I had no idea how to obtain it. We continued to pray. As we approached the 30-day deadline when the contact was set to expire, the realtor called me to see if we had secured financing. Very dejected, disappointed and frustrated, I just laid it out there to him.

"We don't have financing. Every door has closed in front of us. I'm sorry, but I'm not sure what is going to happen."

He said, "The owners have decided to carry a note on the building for you. They want you to put the terms you can afford into a contract and send it over to them."

After I got off the phone I was in awe. These are people we have never met or even spoken to. They don't know anything about us or what we are trying to do. They even had an offer greater than the one we settled on. This has to be God giving us favor.

I immediately called a meeting with some men I knew could help us put this contract together. We sent a contract over and they accepted everything in it with one exception, they wanted 20 percent down.

Here I was again, in an impossible situation. Misty and I continued to pray and seek direction and provision from God for this.

One morning during my devotion time I was reading on sowing and reaping. As I'm listening to the Lord, I heard His voice in my head say, "Plant a seed and expect a harvest."

At first, I was thinking, "Lord I need to save all I can to help come up with the down payment."

But the longer I stayed in prayer, the more impressed I felt. So I called Misty and shared with her what I believed the Lord spoke to my heart.

She said, "Let's do it!"

I figured that by depleting all our savings, we could come up with $10,000 as a seed offering to the Lord. With much expectancy, the next week we planted that seed into our local church. We needed $48,000 at closing to have our 20 percent down, so that was what we believed God for. Two weeks before we were to close on the building, a man whom I knew as an acquaintance walked into my office with a check for $50,000 and said he wanted to pay for our down payment. When he stepped out of my office, I got up, closed my office door and knelt at my chair to thank God.

My faith in God increased big-time! I experienced God in a way that I had never experienced before. He showed me the building He wanted us to have. He walked me through the process of providing for it. He showed me that when man says, "No." God says, "Yes!" And He taught me to be faithful to plant seeds into other ministries and individuals. This is laying up treasures in heaven for the times when we will need it.

So if what you have is not enough, plant a seed. God will bring a harvest from heaven to meet your every need. When you plant your seeds in heaven, it is multiplied. The Kingdom of God is the greatest investment you can ever make.

Go Possess the Land

Three days before we were to close on our building, I get a call from a man named Wes. He was the executive pastor of First Baptist church which was located directly across the street from the building we were purchasing. After some greetings, he asked about our ministry and what we planned to do with the building. I got excited because I just knew he was asking to see how they could partner with us in ministry. So I shared our vision and the amazing things God was already doing. And then I told him that we were going to be neighbors so maybe we should get together for lunch sometime.

He responded, "I won't let you move into that building. We have a daycare across the street and it will not look good to have that type of ministry so close to our client's children."

My emotions completely reversed from joy to anger. I was thinking about how far we had come. We had walked through great trials and now this man wants to tell me he is going to stop God?

So I asked, "Exactly how are you going to stop us from moving into this building?"

He said, "I have already contacted our attorneys and city officials. Trust me, Sir, you are not moving into that building. Save your time and money."

As my blood began to boil, I replied, "Mr. Wes, God has told us to go possess this land. The last time I checked, you are not bigger than God."

This was another valley to cross, another mountain to climb in my mind. But I had a quiet confidence in God that we were following His lead.

So when I got off the phone, I prayed to God and said, "Father, this is Your problem, not mine. I'm doing what You have asked me to do. I'm moving forward with Your assignment for my life."

Not knowing if he was speaking for the whole church or even the senior pastor, I decided to set an appointment with the senior pastor to see where that might lead. We got an appointment and went in to visit with him. The only two items I brought was our newly created brochure of our ministry and my Bible. The brochure was to provide as much information as I could about us and the Bible...well it was to be used in case they wanted to take a closer look at their actions from a Biblical standpoint. I know, I know...I was in the flesh.

But God saved me even from myself because the meeting went well. The pastor was so gracious. I shared with him that we wanted to be good neighbors and were willing to do all that we could to make them feel that way toward us.

His only request was that we would keep in communication with one another in case an issue should arise. I gave my word that we would. He asked me to come down to Wes's office with him for a minute. We walked down the hall into Wes's office. The senior pastor introduced me. I stood in the doorway of his office, nervous and prepared to run if necessary.

The pastor addressed Wes and said, "Everything is fine. We welcome them and look forward to helping them."

Wes sat back down in his chair and that was it. I'm not sure if Wes was taking the lead on this; if the senior pastor asked him to; or if there was an outcry from the church. I didn't know and didn't want to know. I was just totally relieved that we had a good meeting and understanding.

We contacted the City of Longview to have them send an inspector out to see what would need to be done to bring the building up to code. During the inspection we were told that the building was zoned correctly and in great shape. The inspector told us that we would have no problem passing. However, since we were looking to house people in it, it would need a sprinkler and fire alarm system before occupying it. I had no idea what that meant, but God had brought us this far, surely He would complete the work He had begun.

I began checking with several companies that installed these systems, the lowest cost I could find was over $80,000. In faith, I signed a contract and told them to get started as soon as they could. We were going to pay three installments as work was completed. We were trusting that God would supply the funds to cover what we needed. To be honest, it did cross my mind that if He didn't come through, we were sunk! But my faith had increased from all the other miracles God had performed. I just knew that He would be on time with the amount needed. And slowly as people around the community began to hear about our vision, money began coming in and our needs were met.

Chapter Eleven
Our Inner Atlas

"Now the Word of the Lord came to Jonah. . ."[58] Have you ever heard a voice when no one else was near you? Have you ever felt a strong impression to do something and you really didn't even know why? Have you ever read a scripture in the Bible that you have read many, many times but then it suddenly makes sense? If so, that is God speaking to you. The Bible says that "his sheep know His voice."[59] Can you imagine the God of Heaven, the very One that created everything, is speaking to you and me? As unreal as that may seem to the unbelieving in today's society, yes, God did create everything. And yes, this same God communicates with His children.

So how do you know it's God and not just you having a conversation with yourself? The Bible says that "your spirit will agree with His spirit and will be led by Him."[60] There have been many times a thought popped into my mind regarding something I should do or say. But when I was prepared to act on it, or began to pray about it, my spirit grieved within me. I realized what I was doing was not of God but rather an expression of my own thoughts and desires. That is one of the reasons

---

[58] Jonah 1:1
[59] John 10:4
[60] Romans 8:14-16

why I try always to pray and even sleep on a decision before acting on it. I want to give God time to check me. I want to know for sure that God is speaking to me.

I had a growing passion to tell others of my new findings regarding the sovereignty of God. I wanted to shout it from the rooftop because it has helped me so much. I wanted everyone else to receive the same help. But the timing was not right for me to announce to the world what I had learned.

One night before going to bed, I felt a strong impression to write a book on the subject. The title, the chapters and a lot of the content of this book came to me all at once and literally overwhelmed my thinking. I had a very hard time getting to sleep, but I wanted to sleep that night on the idea just to make sure I was not acting out of my own passions.

So I got up the next morning and said to my wife, "Misty, I had a funny feeling last night that I should write a book about the sovereignty of God."

She then told me that a few days before she had the same thought.

I then went to the church and prayed. I asked God to open my ears so I could hear His voice clearly. I told the Lord that I did not want to misrepresent His word or His character. Then, as I always try to do, I shut up, invited His presence, and listened. Obviously you know the outcome because you are reading this book.

God wants to speak to you and give you direction. God will verify the direction He wants you to go and what it is He has spoken to you if you just ask. He understands that you are trying to decipher between your thoughts and His will.

David gives us some insight into this when he says, "the steps of a good man are ordered by the Lord."[61] Most translations replace the word "good" with the word "righteous." But the word that fascinates me the most from this verse is "ordered."

One of Webster's definitions gives the closest relationship to what God means by "ordered." The definition says: "an instruction for a person to follow." As a general commands his soldier, God will speak to you and give directions to follow in this life.

David's son Solomon also writes of God directing us when we pray: "Trust in the Lord with all your heart, lean not on your own understanding. In all your ways acknowledge Him, and He shall direct your paths."[62]

Living a surrendered life unto the Lord will guarantee you an inner atlas on this pilgrimage home. The Holy Spirit is your inner guide.

In John, Jesus explains to His disciples how the Holy Spirit within them will be their guide: "However, when He, the Spirit of Truth, has come, He will guide you into all truth; for He will not speak on His own authority, but whatever He hears He will speak: and He will tell you things to come. He will glorify Me, for He will take of what is Mine and declare it to you. All things that the Father has are mine. Therefore I said that He will take of mine and declare it to you."[63]

So what happens if the Lord has pointed you in a different direction? What if the tugs at your heart and the voice in your head, the words of wisdom and knowledge from your friends, family and pastor are not getting through to you? What if you are enjoying your

[61] Psalms 37:23
[62] Proverbs 3: 5-6
[63] John 16: 13-15

job and making more money than you have ever made so you feel full-time ministry is not an option? What if you grew up in the city and going on the mission field is not an option? What if you cannot even think about putting your kids and wife through "life on the road" while you travel and preach the Word of God?

Well, if God has ordered a change in your location or has given you a task or calling to fulfill, and you ignore the Lord's voice, then He will bring about uncomfortable circumstances to get your attention. And sometimes that is also the cause of the pain you are feeling.

Jonah experienced firsthand God making his circumstances uncomfortable. God spoke to him, giving him a Word for the Ninevite people. Because of his own anger and selfish desire to see them punished, he ran from God's directive.[64] Jonah thought he was justified in his actions. After all, the Ninevites had treated his people wrongly. But God does not see things through our eyes. He has a set of His own.

Jonah's first experience with uncomfortable circumstances was right after jumping on a ship to escape the presence of God (like someone can actually do that). God stirred up a storm and revealed to the men on the boat, through the casting of lots, that Jonah was the problem. After he confessed to them his "fleeing from God" attempt, he found himself thrown overboard.

Jonah's next experience with uncomfortable circumstances was in the belly of a fish. (You have got to give it up to the Lord for creativity on this one.) So God had a large fish swallow Jonah to give him some time to think about his actions and decisions.

Running away from God's will is like trying to run

---

[64] Jonah 1: 1-3

away from your shadow in an open field at noon on a sunny day.

You might say: "Why could He not choose someone else?" You could try, but the same will apply to you as it did to Jonah. God knows best and He knows what you need to fulfill the agenda He has planned just as much as He needs the agenda fulfilled. He knows that it will benefit you just as much as it benefits the purpose He wants accomplished through you.

God's pursuit of Jonah was not so much about Jonah's ability but because of the man, Jonah, himself. Jonah wanted his enemies to suffer. He knew that he served a gracious and good God and that God wanted to show mercy to the Ninevite people. So Jonah was not showing the heart of God toward the people. God created the Ninevites and He wanted them to serve Him. He wanted Jonah to have a changed heart and reconsider his motives and rekindle compassion for the people. That's why it had to be Jonah and no one else.

The same will be true for you. It is not that you are the only one in existence that can solve the problem or minister to a certain need of people. It is that you are the only one in existence at that particular point in time that needs to experience solving the problem or ministering to a certain need.

Your co-workers begin treating you as though you do not belong, start praying and searching your inner atlas. God might have better plans for you. God might know of a new co-worker that needs to come to know Him in a personal way. Your apartment complex is "under new management" and your rent is not affordable anymore, start praying and searching your inner atlas. God might have better plans for you. God might know of a potential new neighbor that needs to come to know Him in a personal way. If your friends are not too friendly anymore, God might have better plans for you. God might be placing you around new people who you can influence in a godly way.

Your spiritual headlights only extend so far. You need a God's-eye view to know what is coming up next for your life. Pray and depend on the Lord. Listen to the Holy Spirit, your inner atlas. In doing so, you will not miss the next mission God has planned for you.

My Pink Cast

While on staff at the church in Virginia, I developed a close friendship with Tom Rosson. Tom was the Mission Director at the church but he only made a two-year commitment because his plans were to raise enough money so he could go back out to the mission field. We stayed in touch and he soon left for Germany. He serves as President of Eurasian Theological Seminary Moscow. He also does a lot of missionary work in Germany, planting churches and establishing ministry schools.

Misty and I began supporting him financially each month because we truly believe in Tom and the work he is doing. I got an email from Tom inviting me to Germany to see him and the work he was doing. I planned my trip and invited Phil and two more friends to join me.

Around this same time, the summer was approaching so we thought it would be a good idea to give our disciples some recreation. We signed up to have a softball team in a church league.

A week before we were to leave on our trip to Germany, we had our first game. Now try to imagine this: Our first game is against a well-known church in our city that is very influential. If you are someone important, or at least think you are someone important, you probably attend this church. Each one of their team members drive into the parking lot in their nice cars. The whole team is in uniform wearing the same jerseys with softball pants, cleats and matching gloves. They all looked tan, healthy, clean and proper.

Now, here we come pulling into the parking lot in our old beat up 15-passenger white van that smokes, and every once in a while will very loudly backfire. A bunch of men get out that have been living on the streets most of their life. They look rough. Most are unshaved. Some have long beards and goatees. All of them have visible tattoos and scars from the street life.

We did get some matching jerseys donated to us, but under the jerseys my guys are wearing blue jeans, cut-off shorts, slacks and anything else they could find. Needless to say, we stood out.

We might not have looked that great but we practiced hard and felt like we had a chance to compete. So our heads were held high and we walked around like we were the greatest thing since sliced bread...until the first inning started. We found out very quickly that we needed more practice. A whole lot more practice, because we got crushed. And that continued for the rest of the season.

During the first game and my first at bat, I hit a single through the infield. My teammate behind me hit a pop fly into the outfield. I'm watching the ball and waiting between first and second base. The ball hits in the outfielder's glove and pops out.

I take off running as fast as I can to second base. On the way there I stepped on something and I hear a pop. So I look back to see what I stepped on but there was nothing there. By the time I made it to second base, I realized what happened. I had either pulled or tore a ligament in my foot. I hopped back to the dug out and as soon as I sat down, pain rushed to my foot like I had not felt before. It felt as if someone had a knife and was going to town stabbing the bottom of my foot. I could not put any pressure on it to walk or even stand. My guys carried me back to my car and Misty drove me home.

I tried everything I could to avoid going to the ER that night but I knew that I needed to get in to see a doctor soon. The next morning I went to a local medical clinic that confirmed what I thought. I had indeed pulled a ligament in the arch of my right foot. The clinic set an appointment with a foot specialist for the next day to get a cast put on. When I got there to get the cast, the nurse tells me that they are out of every color but red for the cast. I was not too fond of having a red cast, but neither did I want to wait and come back another day. Plus, my trip to Germany was now less than two days away, so I couldn't wait. But what the nurse did not bother to tell me was that any exposure to the sun causes the red to quickly fade to pink.

By the time the guys arrived at my house to pick me up to go to the airport, I was wearing a hot pink cast. It took them a while to pick themselves up off the floor from laughter, but finally they gathered their composure enough to help me get my bags in the car.

It's humorous now, but at the time it was embarrassing. And once we landed in Germany, I think it was embarrassing for these guys, too. Because while in Germany for those 10 days, I noticed that in public places they kept their distance from me. But I understood, because I wanted to keep distance from my own foot if it were not attached. Good times!

Ultimatum

We spent 10 days in Europe traveling from place to place. It was a wonderful and insightful experience. On the 14-hour flight back home, I had a lot of time to reflect on our discipleship program, my family and my position at the church. I set some new goals and I was coming home with new energy and excitement.

When I walked into the office doors, my executive secretary met me there. She had a concerned look on her face and said, "Pastor is waiting for you in the conference room."

This was very unusual for many reasons.

First of all, I was always there before he was and on this particular day, I had arrived almost an hour earlier than I normally would have.

Secondly, why the conference room? Normally if just he and I were to meet, it would be in either mine or his office.

Thirdly, the executive secretary, Jennifer, was a dear friend of mine and I could tell something was wrong by the look on her face.

I went to my office, laid down my brief case and went in to see him. He asked how the trip went. I shared that it was good, but kept it very short knowing that those were normal greetings yet there was something else coming.

The pastor then opened his Bible and read from Isaiah

1:18a "come let us reason together." He then pulled his notepad over to him where it appeared he had made a list.

He began to tell me that the discipleship program, the outreaches and even my involvement on the worship team at the church was all a distraction to me. He said that I must end the discipleship program or turn it over to another ministry. I must not do anymore outreaches with our team. And during each service, instead of being involved in leading the worship, playing an instrument or anything else, I was to follow him around because he needed a "buffer" between him and the congregation.

He followed all that up by saying that if I could not give these things up that he could find someone else to do my job. I was given an ultimatum.

I didn't know how to respond. I saw what we were doing as being an extension of the church, not my own thing. I thought that what everyone in the congregation was supposed to be doing was reaching the lost and discipling them to Christ.

After all, the pastor had even preached sermons on that so how better to lead than by example. I thought he would be excited about the people being reached and brought into the church. Everyone was seeing the impact Christ was making in these men's and women's lives.

But all I could say to him was, "I need some time to pray and think about it."

After the meeting, I went straight to the prayer room. I was confused, hurt and desperately in need of Jesus to comfort me. I knew, without any doubt, that God had called me to these ministries. But now I had to make a choice between them.

There were two dynamics at work that brought us to this place – perception and direction.

The first dynamic is that the way I saw these ministries and the way the senior pastor saw these ministries were totally different. I had every intention of helping him fulfill his vision for the church and I saw these ministries as doing that. I had even gone to him many times and asked if we should bring them totally under the covering of the church for more accountability. But he and the board declined due to too much liability. I emailed him reports of what we were doing from time to time so I could keep him informed. I truly believed this was in line with the vision of the church.

However, he perceived that I was trying to do my own thing and that these ministries were distracting me from my job there. You see, I thought I was doing my job by reaching more people and bringing them to the church. He thought I was building my own ministry and taking resources and people away from the church.

The next dynamic is direction. All in all, God just had other plans for my life. I know this senior pastor prays and tries his best to hear from God. I know the men on the board are godly men and truly have the church and the Kingdom of God in mind.

So why did this happen? Where was the breakdown in communication? How did it come to this? God had other plans. Just as I shared previously about our inner atlas, God was working out a divine direction for my life and the church. I didn't understand it. I couldn't see it at the time. But God knew exactly what He was doing and He was leading the hearts of everyone. I know that now, but at the time I had a career-changing, life-altering decision to make.

Funny thing is, the whole time during our meeting while the pastor was laying out his criteria for my employment, I knew in my heart what the right decision was. But I wanted to take the time to hear clearly from the Lord.

A couple of days passed and I was still wrestling with some major thoughts. Misty and I were the primary funding for the ministry. We literally lived off of her income and every penny I made went toward feeding and housing our residents. I was struggling with my calling because I knew that God had called me to lead worship since I was a child, yet I would also have to give that up as well. I struggled with my self-worth because there was no salary to step in to. So I would no longer be providing for my family. All of these thoughts kept me in a state of confusion.

Then I got a call from Pastor James Taylor. Pastor Taylor is one of my mentors who I met with from time to time. I had not spoken to him about these recent developments because I was trying to hear from God myself without any outside influences. Yet again, God had other plans.

He said, "Tim, I'm not sure what you are going to think about this, but I was on the phone with a missionary from New York. Her name is sister Longley. She just got back from oversees and she called me saying that there is someone in my life that she needs to speak with. She described the young man to me and Tim, it is you. You need to call her."

He gave me her number and I immediately called.

When she answered the phone, I said, "Hi. I'm Tim Wiseman a friend of Pastor James Taylor."

Her next word was, "Run!"

I said, "Excuse me?"

She continued, "You need to run as fast as you can away from the situation you are in. I don't know what is going on in your life, but while I was oversees God laid you on my heart and told me to tell you to run away. Jealousy has set in and God has other plans for your life. He is breaking you out of the cell you've been in. Run as a bird that flees from its cage. God has given you a large, vast land. He wants you to develop it for the lost. Go! Run! And don't look back."

She said many more things and I wrote everything she said down. I was in awe. If God was trying to send me a clear message, He definitely got His point across. I had never experienced anything like this before, but I had complete peace in my heart that this was from God.

On Thursday, I decided to fast lunch and go down to our building to pray. I ended up praying longer than I realized and I was late for a media meeting I was to be a part of. As I left the building and looked back, I knew right then that I was going to resign.

I called Misty on the way to the meeting and told her that today is the day.

She said, "I was wondering when you would give in to what God wanted for us."

I just smiled with a complete peace and drove on to the church. As I walked in I could tell that the pastor was upset with me for being late, rightfully so.

When the meeting was over I asked to meet with him for a minute. He agreed and we went to his office. I had already typed up a resignation letter the previous day. I handed it to him and told him that I was resigning. I shared with him that although I thought this is all based on the wrong perception, I also feel that God is moving me on.

I requested two things in the letter. The first was that he allow me to stay for 30 days because I needed to get my finances in order. The second request was, if the church wanted to give me a going away party that they help us with preparing our new building instead.

The pastor acted as though he never saw the resignation coming.

He asked me, "What am I supposed to do if this doesn't work out for you? What am I supposed to say to you when you come back requesting your position back? We are going to move on from here."

I told him, "If I come back to you requesting my position back, you remind me that this is God's will and don't hire me."

He probably thought I was crazy for leaving a good paying, high position in a church to step out into nothing. What he didn't know is, I am a little crazy!

Over the next 30 days, the church embraced my move and was very good to me. I didn't realize how many in the church knew in their heart that this was coming. I told everyone that they are releasing me as a local missionary. There was a strong sense of joy and adventure in my home.

Now don't get me wrong, taking this huge step of faith was scary, especially when you have to make it suddenly with no preparation or warning. You will always have to choose between the facts verses faith. Did I make the right decision? Did I do it too early?

I remember my first day down this new pathway. It was Monday morning. The same routine I had for over 15 years of waking up, doing my devotions, fixing coffee and heading into the office was over. I had no office to go to. I spent the whole day in my bedroom crying, praying and feeling lost. I didn't know what to do.

Tuesday, I was in better shape emotionally, but still lost. I spent the better part of the day in my room crying and praying, but I did go down to teach a class to my residents later in the evening.

We are taught by society that the only certainties that we have are the ones that we make for ourselves. We look for job security to have certainty that our financial needs and even wants will be met. We pay for our home, car(s), and other items to ensure that we'll always have a roof over our head and transportation. We look for certainty in insurance that it will replace our assets if something should happen. But, is there really any certainty in any of those?

Look at the trial of Job. He had everything stripped from him in one day. Everything he had worked so hard to accumulate, that he thought would bring certainty in his life, gone. What does true certainty look like? What is certain in life? In this life, absolutely nothing is a sure thing. The only certainty we have is our relationship with God. Our only certainty is our trust in a God who is faithful to meet every one of our needs according to His riches and glory, not ours.

Wednesday morning I asked God if I had made the right decision. I will never forget what God told me, "Not only did you make the right decision, but I'm excited about your future."

Wow! God excited about my future? That put a smile on my face that stayed for days.

Trying to Please Man

The elders board of the church requested that I come in to address them on some questions they had. Out of respect for them and how good they had been to me over the years, I attended. During the meeting there were questions of whether I would continue going to the church or leave. I told them that I planned to attend the church and continue to support the church in any fashion I could.

There was a question raised by an elder before the meeting as to whether my true motivation was to start my own church and pull people out.

When I heard about this, I broke down into tears, hurt that someone would even bring up that accusation against me. But I promised the elders that I would continue to go to the church and would continue to serve. And that God had not called me to pastor a church so I would not be pulling anyone from the church. I also assured them that I was not doing anything to hurt the church.

This ended up coming back to bite me on the backside. The Bible specifically says that we are not to say what we will do tomorrow for we do not know what tomorrow holds. Only God knows the future (James 4:13-15). We are to say "if the Lord wills" when we say anything about what we will do in the future. In my attempt to please man, I committed myself to something I could not fulfill. God had other plans for my life that I was not aware of at the time. Also, I did not heed to the words the Lord spoke to me through Sister Longley, "Run!"

I tried to fix things myself. I tried to squash the accusations already forming, not knowing that I was about to make them a lot worse. And I did not preface my promise to stay at the church with "if the Lord wills." This was a big mistake and would be held against me.

A week passed and Lee Bates, one of the pastors from First Baptist Church, called me to see if I could lead worship for them on a Sunday morning. This is the same church that I initially had, well let's say, intense "fellowship" with one of their leaders.

I thought, "One Sunday being gone from my church will not hurt anything." So I emailed the pastor letting him know that I would be gone. After I led worship, Lee approached me and asked if I could fill in a little longer until they found someone. I agreed and led worship there two more Sundays.

Then Lee approached me again and said that the church wanted to make me interim worship leader until they found someone. Now I knew I needed to make a decision. So I prayed and the Lord clearly showed me that He had opened this door for my family. This church was going to give me a stipend for leading worship and this would help me to build a good relationship with my neighbor.

Also, God was using me in my calling to lead in worship which is something I was not able to do before.

Knowing this was the Lord opening this door, I just knew He would show the church I had resigned from that this is a good temporary move for my family. So I contacted the elders and pastor to let them know what was happening in my life. Immediately all the accusations were validated in their minds.

The "I told you so" began to fly off some of the people's lips. Suddenly, "Tim is not a man of his word." "Tim is a liar." "Tim betrayed the church and the pastor."

Once again, their perception was one thing. My honest intention to follow God was another. I just continued moving forward trying to follow the plan God laid out for my life. I decided to anchor down, be still and be quiet. God was my defender and there was no reason to defend myself. I accepted the position and led worship there for several months. Misty and I built many relationships there and formed a great relationship with the church leadership.

I learned many lessons through these events. But the greatest one was that I did not need to defend myself. Anytime you take a step of faith, you can expect adversity. It's not against any person that we are wrestling against; it's the enemy of our soul trying his best to stop the work God is doing in us and through us. Satan will deceive others into believing their own perception, rather than reality. Satan will use people to hurt you.

Think about Joseph and his brothers; David's own son Absalom; Job and his friends; and Jesus and the people He came to save. Always keep your eyes on Jesus and know that He is your defender.

Since that time, many of the same people who brought accusations against me have come back to me and apologized. Although I had already forgiven them, it just showed me that God is the Restorer of relationships. We don't have to fix or patch anything. There are some relationships that you may want, but God knows they are unhealthy for you. Those He will not restore and even prevent you from having. That doesn't mean each party cannot forgive and move on. That just means that God has a new season of relationships for you. When you see new people coming into your life, you are entering into a new season. Embrace it and move on with those people. God is doing a new thing!

Chapter Twelve
God Still Performs Miracles

To this day I cannot explain to you how it happened, but even without Misty and me contributing regularly to the ministry, all of our needs were being met by various people in the community. We always had just enough to pay our bills. The best way I can describe it is like it was manna, rained down from heaven that was sufficient for that day.

The installation for the sprinkler system continued. Then we got our first bill for it – $19,000. To me that amount seemed insurmountable, but God had met our needs before and we believed he would do it again. The next day a bill came in from the city for $3,900 for a water tap needed for the sprinkler system. Now the work had stopped until these bills could be paid.

We continued to pray and ask God to open doors for us to present our ministry to people who could support us financially. Just at the right time, we received a gift for the exact amount we needed to move forward. So we called everyone to continue on with the work.

During this time, we would commute back and forth each day. We stayed at our homes in the evening and spent the days working on our new facility and teaching classes to our men.

One day the Fire Marshall came by and told us that

we could not hold our classes there in the building, we could only do construction work. He said that classes would be considered occupying the building. God met this need the very same day by First Baptist allowing us to use their classrooms in their recreation building. God just kept on meeting our needs and everything seemed to be moving forward.

On Monday nights, I started bringing all the men to my house to watch Monday night football and, during half-time, we would turn off the TV for a devotion.

A man named Wayne began coming over to teach the devotion. Wayne had contacted my dad and asked if we needed any teachers to volunteer. Wayne was also the administrator for a recovery ministry in a nearby town. The men really enjoyed his teaching. He had served 14 years in prison and had been addicted to drugs for most of his life. Wayne could relate to the men and their struggles.

Around this same time, Chris asked to meet with me and Phil. We met at a coffee shop one evening and he expressed to us that he wanted to start his own recovery ministry. He said that he had the financial backing from some people and saw it as a great opportunity for us to meet the needs of more people.

I didn't feel in my heart that it was the right timing for Chris, I felt there was more he needed to learn. But there's no doubt that Chris carried more potential to be a great leader than any who had come into our program. So we committed to supporting him in prayer and told him that we would contribute $1,000 to help him get started.

When Wayne found out that we needed someone to run our program, he began inquiring about the position.

We interviewed him, prayed about the decision and after a couple of weeks hired him as our program director. We knew right away that he was sent by God. Wayne was a very hard working man and he quickly whipped our program into shape. I was impressed and thankful to God for sending him just at the right time.

We continued to move forward with getting the building ready for occupancy. We received the final two bills of $14,979 and $33,000 for the alarm and sprinkler system. We continued to pray and keep our faith in God. He had met our needs up to this point; we were confident this time would be no different.

However, it was different this time. Enough finances came in to pay the $33,000 on time, but there were no more funds to pay the $14,979. So we waited, watched and prayed for God to open doors for us to meet people to whom we could present the ministry.

A month passed by and the company began to call and ask where their money was. Another month passed by and the company kept calling wanting their money. I reminded them that before they ever started on this project, I was transparent with them and that we did not have the money but we were going to raise it as we went along. Evidently they forgot all about the conversation, because they then sent us a letter letting us know that we had 30 days from the date on the letter to pay in full or they were going to stop monitoring our alarm system and send us to collections.

I knew that if we lost our monitor for our alarm, we would also lose our occupancy with the city. Now we have urgency in our prayers. I'm still going out to the community, meeting people and trying to bring awareness to our need. But everyone I presented the ministry would just say, "Thank you for coming by." Nothing else!

Now it was 20 days and counting. Not one penny came in. Ten days to go and still, not one cent. Six days before we lose our building and occupancy, I'm sitting at a local restaurant when my phone rings. It was one of the pastors from First Baptist Church.

"Hey man, I had lunch today with a member of our church," he says. "He's a local businessman and he was inquiring about your ministry and asked a lot of questions about it. He also showed interest in supporting you guys. Be watching for his phone call and let me know how it turns out."

As I thanked him and hung up the phone, the businessman calls me. He explained to me that he recently got an unexpected return on an investment he made.

"I don't need it so why don't you stop by my office later to pick it up," he says. "It's for $15,000. I hope you can use it."

"You have no idea! Thank you so much!" I said.

I yelled "Praise God!" in the middle of the restaurant. Everyone looked at me weird, but I did not care.

I got the check and deposited it. As Misty is writing the check to the company to pay our final bill, the company calls wanting to know when we can pay them.

We tell them, "The check is in the mail."

Four days after mailing the check to them, they call back telling us that we overpaid on the last bill because they forgot we were a non-profit organization and added taxes. They mailed back to us a check for $3,000. Isn't God amazing?

After the sprinkler system was complete and paid for, we called in city inspectors and began finalizing everything for our occupancy. After a few minor improvements to our building, we got our Certificate of Occupancy and moved in!

Blueprint

When we were created, God placed a call and assignments on our life. The call is to come to know Christ and be conformed to His likeness. The assignments for our life are when we stay surrendered to Him and allow Him to lead us. He will then tell us where we need to be; when we need to be there; and what we are supposed to do upon arrival.

Now we have dominion over this world. So we have the right to fulfill this assignment or not to fulfill it. God will not interfere with us. In His providence, He gave us authority and dominion. He is not a micro-manager. He will not intervene unless we invite Him to do so.

So let's say that you have accepted your purpose and assignment and are ready to get to work for our Savior. Let's consider our assignments as blueprints for us to follow. Now, God hands us the blueprint and tells us to go build this house. He tells us that everything we need – all our materials and supplies – will be ready and delivered at the moment we need them and we request and pray for them. In addition to this, He promises to be right beside us working and helping all along the way.

At this point is where I have gotten it wrong many times. And I believe many others do, also. We begin looking at the house our neighbor is building. We start staring at their blueprint. Jealousy and envy set in. We begin to wonder why we can't have a house like theirs, instead of staying focused on our blueprint and the house God has given to us to build.

Another mishap, we try to order material ahead of it's time. Timing is everything in the Kingdom of Heaven. God will not allow us to get ahead of the process. When we need the material for the foundation, it will be there upon request. But if all we need is the material for the foundation, but we are requesting material for the roof already, God will not supply that material yet.

He will respond, "Look at your blueprint. You are not there yet. Finish the task I have before you right now. I will supply for the roof when it comes time. For now, finish the foundation."

I made this mistake early in my ministry. I began looking at how other ministry centers were running. I saw the large amount of ministry taking place and began asking God for the same for us. He knew that I couldn't handle it at the time, so He did not answer my prayer. And I'm thankful He did not. He wanted me to stay focused on building the foundation of this discipleship program first.

Matthew 18:18 teaches us about binding and loosing. Binding is a contractual agreement between two people or organizations. Binding is bringing the two together into a bond agreement. Every action and agreement we make here on earth will be made in heaven. God desires for us to fulfill our agreements. We have the authority to make decisions over our domain and those decisions will be secured in the Kingdom of Heaven.

I believe one of the reasons our prayers go unanswered is two-fold. First of all, it's not the right timing. We have not reached the point in the process that requires our need to be met. Just because it looks desperate to us and we feel we have got to have it right now, doesn't mean that God is in Heaven panicking and trying to figure out how to get the answer to us. He knows the process better than we do. He is telling us to wait and stay focused on building and complete the task we currently have at hand.

Secondly, we ask for things that are not in our domain. We want what someone else has instead of building what God has before us. We want the same fireplace our neighbor has instead of being content with the fireplace God has for us. We want the same color brick he or she has across the street instead of trusting God and building what He wants. It's all His anyway. We must stay in the process God has for us. And we must stay content with what God has for us.

In the body of Christ, some are called to be the head. If you are the arm, stop trying to be the head. God also gives some 30-, some 60-, some 100-fold. If God has only given you 30, stop getting upset that you don't have the 100. It's part of His blueprint for your life. If God has only given you only one talent, stop getting upset that you don't have the 10 talents. He gives each of us a measure of faith according to His scales and weights. He did not have to give us anything at all. As a matter of fact, He did not have to create us. We are His to do with as He pleases.

Keep your hands busy with what God has given you. Come to a place of rest and contentment. Follow your own blueprint for your life. He will do more than you could ever dream up for your life. You will live an adventure-filled life full of excitement and abundance. That's what your blueprint looks like.

The Cookie Monster

Although we had all our bills paid in full and now had our occupancy, we had nothing left in the bank. Misty came to me and said that she checked our account and we only had $8 in it as of that morning. I asked Misty to look up what our regular contributions had been over the last 90 days to gauge if we could make budget. She did and it wasn't even close to what we needed. Our financial needs were around $4,000 a month at this time and we only had about $1500 a month being contributed. And the $1,500 had already come in for the month which left us no money for the next three weeks.

I called Phil and said, "Brother, you need to start praying with me because we need another miracle for our men to even eat this week."

He agreed to pray with me. The next day I got a call from Robby Duncan. Robby owned a tow-truck company. He said that a truck had a wreck on the highway and they towed the tractor trailer back to his shop. He said it had caught fire but he thought a lot of the merchandise was still in good shape.

Then he asked, "Are you guys interested in some cookies?"

I started thinking, well it's not the healthiest thing in the world, but I guess it will do for my men. "Sure! We'll take all you'll give us."

I called Phil to go out to his shop to look at it. Phil calls me back and says that the damage was minimal on the nose of it, but the cookies were in great shape. He said they were packaged and sealed where no smoke had compromised or damaged them.

So I call Robby to see what we needed to do next.

Robby said, "How 'bout I bring the trailer over to your place and you can sort it out from there."

Not knowing what I was getting myself into, I said, "Bring it on over, partner."

I was still not thinking of a huge trailer, rather a small box trailer, maybe 10- to 15- foot long. No! Robby pulls up with a 58-foot-long trailer. This trailer took up several parking places in the back of our building. Phil and I stood there scratching our heads wondering what in the world we were going to do with all of those cookies.

We decided that the first thing we needed to do was figure out what we had. We asked our men to start unloading them and sorting them in our chapel. Milford was in charge of keeping the inventory. It took us a few days to unload and count all the boxes of cookies we had. I found myself letting God know that He made a big mistake. I thought for sure that He had misunderstood my prayer when I said, "Lord, it would be sweet if You would send us enough money to meet budget this month." I was thinking that He only heard the word "sweet." We learned that we had 12,000 packages of cookies.

The first thing we did was give away as many cookies as we could to local missions that feed or give away food.

My dad also had an idea. Since he was getting a lot of local restaurants and grocery stores to donate food for us, he loaded up a few boxes of cookies to see if we could sell them to the stores. It worked! We started making small deliveries to stores around our city and it was bringing in a few hundred dollars each delivery.

Then Johnny had an idea to contact a local merchant

he knew that owned several drug stores around Texas. We sent him over a list of our inventory and he placed an order for 1,200 packages to be delivered to one of his stores. He bought them from us for $1 and was going to sell them for $.99 to move them quickly. The first day he sold out. He then placed another order for 1,200 more at that location and he wanted to buy 2,400 more to be delivered to two more stores.

Johnny called a radio host he knew and asked her to make an announcement over the radio to go to this drugstore and buy cookies to support our cause. Phil was running a little late getting all 2,400 packages of cookies into our 15-passenger van. The store was in Tyler so he had to driver 45 minutes to get there. When he pulled up to the back of the store, a few workers were waiting on him and telling him to hurry up.

Puzzled, he asked "Why?"

One of the workers said, "Go up front and look for yourself."

So as they are running around trying to get everything stacked onto a pallet, Phil walks up to the front wondering what all the commotion was about. He noticed a long line that extended from the middle of the store all the way outside. He went back to ask the worker what was going on.

"They heard the announcement on the radio and are all here waiting to buy your cookies."

We not only made budget for that month, we ended up selling enough cookies to make budget for the next three months, too. I learned that you have to look for God in every open door. You never know how He will meet your needs. Sometimes He likes to get creative and send you a bunch of cookies.

Disciple Times

"Everyday is a miracle." This is a common theme among us at House of Disciples. It's a miracle that God would use a foolish, wretched man like me to advance His Kingdom. It's a miracle that we have always had the finances to pay our bills. It's a miracle that a man would come into our program and receive help. Especially with all the luring temptations this world offers. It's a miracle that Jesus saves us. And Jesus, himself, is a miracle to us. The fact that all we have to do is believe in Him as our personal Savior, and we are redeemed from every sin – that's a miracle.

Today, House of Disciples is a multiple-city ministry. God has given us a vision for even more ministry centers across America. Our food ministry serves over 30,000 meals a year to people in need. We have an inventory of clothes that fills about 6,000 square feet that we give away to those in need. We started an internship program for our graduates to enter if they want to pursue ministry full-time to earn a degree. To date, we have hired six of our program graduates as staff.

Remember the White Chocolate outreach team? We are involved in over 80 ministry opportunities a year. We now have a strong prison ministry across Texas. We now have six albums that we give away to all the people at our outreach events. We have an album we recorded in the Ferguson Unit prison.

Remember Jimmy? He graduated from our program, became an intern, and now serves as a Program Director at our Madisonville location. From homeless and hopeless, to giving others a home and hope.

Remember Mac? He is still with us today. He has

been free from his addiction for over two years now. Mac walks very closely to God. Now he comes to me to give me words of encouragement all the time.

Our Program Director in Longview came to us as an atheist. He received Christ while in our program. He graduated and stayed with us for training and now leads others to Christ constantly. Chris came back to us and is now working with our program guys in many facets.

Milford lived under a bridge, severely addicted to alcohol. Now he is our program administrator for all locations. These are just a few stories out of many, many more of how God has used House of Disciples to reach and restore people's lives.

Please continue to pray for Donald, James and Lamont. We still minister to them.

Summary

Let's say that instead of embracing my brokenness early on, I got angry at God and blamed all my struggles on him. Would there be an outreach team that sees countless people give their hearts to the Lord every year?

Let's say that instead of allowing compassion to enter my heart for prisoners, I threw my fist at God in anger when my brother was sentenced to prison. Would we be going into prisons across Texas seeing countless men encouraged by the message of grace?

Let's say that instead of believing that there is purpose in my pain, that I believed it was just Satan having his will with me while laughing and pointing his crooked finger saying, "Ha! What are you going to do about it?" Would there be a House of Disciples that has helped countless street people find freedom from addiction?

There is a saying among those who trade on the stocks market: "With knowledge, there is power."

There is an empowering that comes with the knowledge of God's sovereignty. Understanding God's sovereignty will enrich your life and cause you to see your trials in a new perspective. Your faith/trust in God will increase when you surrender your life to Him. You will see the attacks by the enemy of your soul as an opportunity for change. You will see tests as opportunities to grow and become a greater servant. You will see your trials as an opportunity for your weaknesses to be revealed and strengthened by God.

The Word of God is a progressive Word. God created us to be a progressive people. If you have not done so already, please change the way you see your Father-child relationship. Know within your heart that God, your Father, is sovereign. Know that God, your Father, has great plans for your life. And know that your Father loves you so much that He is willing to help you reach your full potential in this life.

So to answer the questions posed at the beginning of this Summary – I don't believe we would be accomplishing what we are now had I not believed that there was purpose in the pain.

About the Author

Tim Wiseman and his wife Misty are the leaders of the House of Disciples in Longview, Texas, where they care for homeless street people through Wiseman Ministries, Inc.

In July of 2008, while living in Longview, Tim and Misty began taking homeless men off the streets and into their home to disciple them in the Christian faith and give them hope that through Christ they could change their lives.

Within a few weeks, the living room in their home became a dormitory with five or six guys living there. Soon thereafter, Tim rented a house where the men could live and, within days, 12 men were living there. So he and Misty took a huge step of faith and rented another house that would take care of 20.

In 2009, Tim founded Wiseman Ministries and purchased the former Welch Funeral Home in Longview, a 12,000-foot facility where they could provide housing and ministry to all the men from the other two houses and many others. The new building also provided more ministry opportunities.

"Every day is a miracle," Tim says of the faith ministry. "Only God could have brought us this far."

Tim was born in 1973 in Memphis, Tennessee, to Roy and Joy Wiseman, faithful servants of the Lord.

"My parents taught my brother and me to give ourselves to others who are in need," Tim says. "They were truly the greatest servants I have ever known."

Tim, who has a bachelor's degree in music composition, has served in full-time ministry since 1996. He was the worship pastor at the New Life Worship Center in Waxahachie, Texas, and also served churches in Longview, Mesquite, Texas, and in Virginia.

While serving in Mesquite, he founded an outreach team to go into areas where homeless people live.

"The objective was to go in and love them," he said. "The outreach team later became known as White Chocolate because of the style of music we were playing."

God has abundantly blessed the ministry and today they have another outreach center for the homeless in Madisonville, Texas, and a large thrift store in Longview. They presently are praying about opening another outreach center in Shreveport, Louisiana.

Tim and Misty worship at the Pathway Church in Longview. They have three children Silas, Malachi and Emma.

More Exciting
StoneGate Books*

The Rise and Fall of Practically Everything asks several pertinent questions: Are we in America on the verge of losing our once-great civilization? Will America become just another great nation that failed? Is this "home of the brave" on a perilous journey to the dust bin of history? What about Oprah Winfrey's new religion? Are the so-called "secular progressives" trying to drive the Christian religion out of the public square and Christians to the back of the bus? What is happening to the "Late Great American Church?" *(Available at www.Stonegatebooks.com)

The Prayer Bag and Other Stories that Warm the Heart takes the reader on a spiritual journey through the prayer lives of some of the greatest Christians the world has ever known... a missionary in the jungles of Sumatra who prayed for a nail and found one; a survivor of the dread Ravensbruck Concentration Camp in Germany who prayed for a brutal guard who brutalized her sister while in the camp; an evangelist who witnessed to Emperor Hirohito of Japan after World War II; and a preacher who carried a cross around the world. "And you will read about my dear wife Vivian Marie who carries a prayer bag with her everywhere she goes."

Joy Comes in the Morning is the true story of one of the greatest miracles of the Twentieth Century. Delores Winder, a Presbyterian lady, was an invalid for 19 years and was planning her funeral when God intervened in her life. She was completely healed during a United Methodist Church Conference on the Holy Spirit in Dallas, Texas, in 1975. Since that time she and her husband Bill have traveled throughout the world telling the amazing story of God's miracle in her life.

The Magic Bullet is a novel about a scientist who discovers the secret of life extension. However, the discovery creates all kinds of problems for him. A recluse billionaire in Chicago – who is dying – wants to find the secret and sends his men to kidnap the scientist. Also, the Chinese government hires a New York City *Mafia don* to find the scientist and learn the secret. The scientist hides out in the Barataria swamps below New Orleans and joins a motorcycle gang en route to the biker's rally at Sturgis, South Dakota, where he is captured by the billionaire's men and taken to Chicago. The reader will laugh and cry but will never forget the dramatic climax.

Gettin' Old Ain't for Sissies is a motivational/inspirational book to help the baby boomers and older survive and enjoy the senior years. The thesis is: "Old age doesn't have to be the end of the line. It can be a bright new beginning." The book outlines the five things a person must do to live a vigorous lifestyle into the 70s, 80s and even the 90s and gives numerous examples of Older Champions.

The Commissioner is the intriguing true story of death and deception and reveals a corrupt political battle during the 1970s that threatened Shreveport, Louisiana. The city's police commissioner – the most powerful lawman in the state – was behind multiple scandals including racism, payoffs, theft of city funds and tampering with a grand jury. He may also have been involved in the murder of an advertising executive who was scheduled to testify against him in court. *(Published by Pelican Publishing Co. and distributed by StoneGate. Available at your local book store)*

Days of Anguish, Days of Hope is the heroic story of Chaplain Robert Preston Taylor who spent 42 months in Japanese prison camps during World War II. On Dec. 7, 1941, the Japanese bombed Pearl Harbor and Manila, the Philippines, the next day. Taylor was caught in a maelstrom of war and the every-day fight for survival. He ministered to the fighting men on the front lines during the Battle for Bataan and received the Silver Star for bravery. He endured the Bataan Death March – where thousands of American soldiers died – the Cabanatuan Prison Camp, and the so-called "hell ships" that were bombed by American pilots who did not know the American prisoners were on board. During the nearly four years in prison, he faithfully ministered God's love to the other prisoners. After he was liberated, he returned home to learn that his wife Ione, who was told he had died on the "hell ships," had remarried. He decided to remain in the military and years later President John F. Kennedy named him Air Force Chief of Chaplains with the rank of major general.